PETER BROCK

CELEBRATING THE LIFE OF A LEGEND THROUGH HIS OWN
POSSESSIONS, AND THE PHOTOS, STORIES AND INSIGHTS OF HIS
FAMILY, FRIENDS AND THOSE WHO KNEW HIM BEST.

PETER BROCK – THE MAN

AFFIRM press

A Cataloguing-in-Publication entry is available from the catalogue of the National Library of Australia at www.nla.gov.au.

ISBN: 9781922213372 (hbk)

First published by Affirm Press in 2012
This revised edition published by Affirm Press in 2014
28 Thistlethwaite Street
South Melbourne, Victoria 3205
www.affirmpress.com.au

Design by Iconic Treasures Pty Ltd and D'fine Creative
Text Copyright © 2012 Beverley Brock, Peter Brock
Printed in China through the Australian
Book Connection

Peter Brock (Icon Series)
Under License by Famed Retail Pty Ltd
Copyright © Famed Retail Pty Ltd 2012
9 Meaden Street, Southbank, Vic 3006

Photographs provided by family members and friends (all supplied from the personal collection of Beverley Brock, unless otherwise stated). All reasonable effort has been made to attribute copyright and credit to individual photographers, and any new information supplied will be included in subsequent editions.

Thanks to the family members of Peter G Brock who contributed to this project: Beverley Brock, James Brock, Robert Brock, Alexandra Summers, Neil Brock, and Sandy Brock.

Thanks for the contributions of Neil Crompton, Bruce Garland, Phil Munday, Peter Daicos, Paul Blair, Ross Mckenzie, Alan Gow, Stanley Toh, Craig Lowndes, Andrew Gaze, Ian Tate, Nick Hluszko, Craig Fletcher, Lou Pruneau, Laurie Lawrence, Jack Brabham, Peter Champion, Graheme Brown (Mort), Richard Leonard, Jim Richards, Ron Walker, Grant Steers, John Sheppard, Ranald MacDonald and David Whitehead.

Special thanks to Beverley Brock for all the time and effort put into helping resource this book.

Editor's note: This publication is a celebration of Peter Geoffrey Brock's (AM) life through memorabillia, photographs and quotes by Peter Brock taken from video footage, newspaper clippings, and personal notes written by Peter Brock.

CONTENTS

Peter Brock has been proclaimed by his peers

and motor racing aficionados as Australia's Number 1 Touring Car Driver of all time, Number 2 World Touring Car Driver, and rated number 14 in the All-Time Greatest Drivers in the World. But Peter was far more than that. He saw motor racing as only 10% of who he was, and he dared to step outside the bounds of motor racing to embrace the wider community.

The adoring public came to know every facet of his racing life and yet he remained a very private person, a man recognised by all but known by few. Women loved him, men immortalised him and a generation have named their children after him.

Jeremy Clarkson, in his documentary on 'Speed', captured the essence of what most leading drivers who push themselves to their limits are really like – quiet, deep thinkers away from the racetrack. Peter's art was exceptional. He loved nature and philosophy. He was also driven by the need for

perfection and was incredibly capable in virtually everything he undertook. Peter examined all things spiritual and loved nothing more than retreating into his private world to regroup in preparation for his next foray into the demanding world of motor sport.

This book is a rare and beautiful insight into the totality of the man, and provides intimate insight into who Peter really was, while still respecting his privacy.

Peter saw himself as an ordinary bloke, 'Brocky', who just happened to have an alter ego known as Peter Brock. To his kids he was simply Dad, to the public he was 'Peter Perfect', to his team he was the boss. Each was simply a facet of the total charismatic, easygoing, talented and complex man.

Wherever possible, we have used Peter's own words. Throughout his life Peter did many interviews on so many aspects of his public life, and also recorded several private audio and video tapes. We have added to his personal perspective by getting a number of people close to Peter to share their recollections and memories of their relationship with him.

These personal insights by family, friends, staff and associates make this collection unique – a genuine, firsthand overview of the man they called 'perfect' (although this description always brought an embarrassed smile to his face).

We hope you enjoy this journey into the personal arena of an exceptional and talented individual who was, after all, a human like the rest of us. He was his own harshest critic. A mere mortal who needed to be loved and thus pushed himself to incredible limits so that he could feel worthy of the adoration the public showered on him.

Beverley Brock

Above – Peter with Dad, Geoff, and the Birana – a brief fling with open wheelers – he saw they didn't get the support of the Aussie fans, so there was no future in driving them.

CHAPTER ONE

BIRTH OF A LEGEND

"I was a real daredevil. I would take on any dare the kids used to give me but it was cars that really got me as a kid. I remember the first car I ever got."

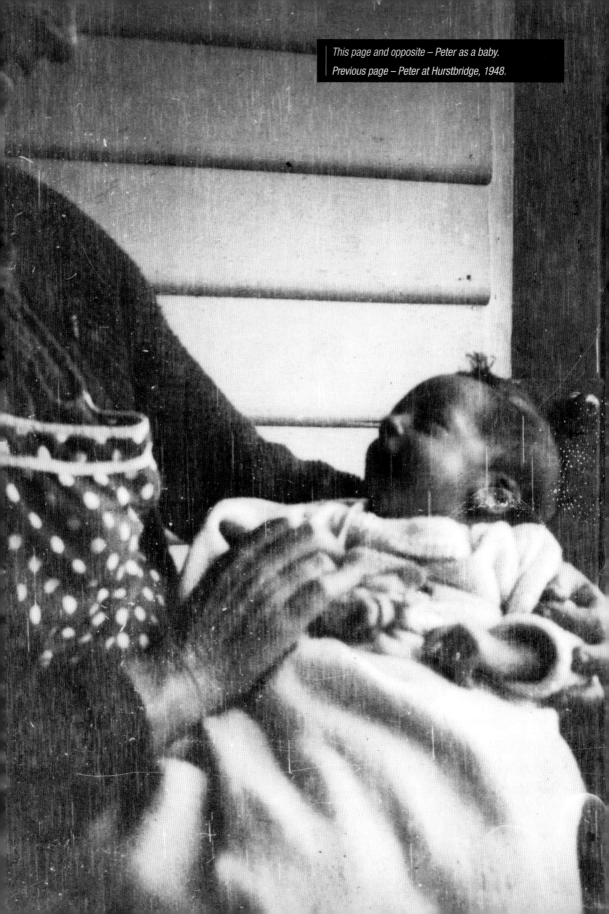

"I was fortunate enough to have a father who supported me no matter what I did, who allowed me to be myself, and a mother who instilled in me a sense of achieving a goal."

Peter Brock

"On February 26th in 1945, Enid Ruth Brock gave birth to her second son, Peter, at the Epworth Hospital in Richmond, Victoria. Ruth and Geoff ended up producing four lively sons. The eldest being Neil, followed by Peter, Lewis and Phil.

The family lived close to their extended family in the Hurstbridge area. Life was simple and funds were scarce. There was no power or running water but there was a supportive, dynamic family environment that encouraged outdoor activity and self responsibility.

The brothers spent a good deal of their time with their cousins, aunt, uncles and grandparents on the family farms in Nutfield and the adjoining Doreen. They made close friendships with the other kids in Hurstbridge and, when not in school, they spent most of their waking hours riding bikes, building billy carts, fishing and swimming. It was an idyllic life in so many ways and Peter's love of the district remained, no matter what heights life took him to."

Beverley Brock

"I was born and bred in a little Victorian country town called Hurstbridge, and my family didn't have a whole lot of money.

When I was growing up I think I was a wildly enthusiastic child. I was into running the fastest, jumping the highest and if someone gave me a double dare, I'd take it.

Fortunately my parents allowed me to be me and although they surely despaired sometimes at the risks I took, I would have to say I owe them a great deal of debt because they allowed me to explore life without any sense of guilt or recrimination.

We spent most of our childhood outside and came home in the evening for dinner. There were no concerns in those days about safety, maybe there should have been because we got up to some pretty crazy stunts, but somehow we all survived without any real serious injuries."

Peter Brock

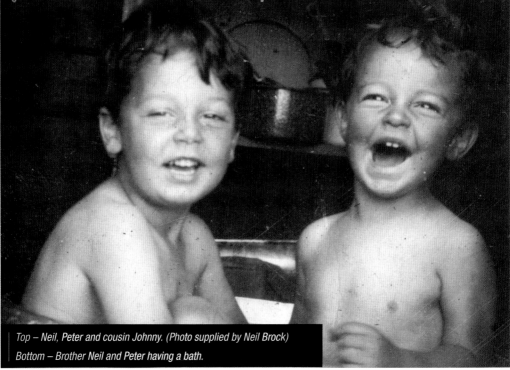

Top – Neil, Peter and cousin Johnny. (Photo supplied by Neil Brock)
Bottom – Brother Neil and Peter having a bath.

Top – Neil and Peter Brock.

Bottom left – Peter, holding baby Lewis and John Brock. (Photo supplied by Neil Brock)

Bottom right – Little cowboys, Peter and Neil Brock.

"Growing up in Hurstbridge during

the 1950s was uncomplicated, and in many ways quite idyllic. Located just 35km from Melbourne, services and amenities were in short supply. One existing service, however, was the electric rail service which connected us to Melbourne. We lacked electricity, reticulated water, and sewerage. Street lights consisted of three 'Tilley' kerosene lamps hung in the main street each night.

The 'ice man' delivered ice for our ice chest, the forerunner to the refrigerator. Milk was delivered by the milkman using a horse cart and decanted into our 'billy'. Telephone was connected via a manual telephone exchange with telephone operators providing the service to other subscribers. Water was used sparingly because our tank's supply was limited (baths once a week). Without sewerage or septic, we had a weekly visit from the 'nightcart' to remove our lavatory pan. We kids were fearful that one of us might be caught on the toilet seat at the time of pan removal.

After-school entertainment was up to us. We roamed the hills nearby and swam in the Diamond Creek or at Bourke's dam. We did however have pictures (movies) in the Hurstbridge Hall and American Westerns influenced some of our after-school activities.

Top – (Left to right) The four boys Peter, Neil holding baby Phillip and Lewis, 1950. (Photo supplied by Neil Brock)

Opposite left – Brothers Neil and Peter, 1948.

Opposite right – (Left to right) Brothers Neil, Peter, Phillip and Lewis Brock, 1953. (Photo supplied by Neil Brock)

The Primary School was 3 doors from our house and we all attest to the very positive, lifelong influence of our Headmaster, Mr Ted Griffiths.

Dad at the time was partner in Hurstbridge Motors with Bill Hale, selling petrol, servicing and repairing vehicles. Dad had an enduring interest in things mechanical all his life, a trait inherited by Peter. Dad also repaired broadcast radios and installed 32-volt lighting plants throughout the district. He was very active in the Hurstbridge Progress Association as well as being President of the School Committee for many years.

Mum was a full-time mum except when playing tennis. She played with a club at Eaglemont (Melbourne suburb) and was an accomplished player and very competitive. I'm sure Peter's competitiveness in part was genetic. In addition, Mum's father, Bill Laidlay, was a renowned local cricketer.

Another regular family activity was attending the then VFL matches. We were all 'one-eyed' Collingwood supporters. It was on these trips from Hurstbridge to suburban Melbourne that Peter's reputation of being 'car mad' was further enhanced. He was able to name virtually every make and model of car we encountered on the way.

Dad had always been interested in motor racing. At that time, I remember us attending meetings at Altona, and the Rob Roy Hillclimb.

Apart from friends, extended family played a huge part in our lives. Both sets of grandparents, the Brocks and the Laidlays were farmers. The farms were located at Doreen and Arthurs Creek, just 15 minutes from Hurstbridge. Numerous holidays were spent at both farms. In addition to holidays, we spent most Sunday afternoons at the Brock farm, which was then known as 'Kirkliston' (the location of our family's Scottish roots).

Also living on the farm in a separate house were Uncle Sandy and Aunty Norma, both of whom have influenced our lives greatly. Our other uncles and aunts with their children (our cousins) came as well. We would engage in various activities including firewood gathering, rabbiting, providing our grandfather, 'Boss,' with free labour to dig

potatoes, pick tomatoes, and gather any other seasonal vegetables.

We'd also celebrate birthdays and family occasions here. Both Peter and I learned to drive at the farm and it was where Peter's now famous Austin 7 made its debut.

Boss and Dad were keen trout fisherman, and their favorite venue was the old Lake Eildon. When the Lake was raised to its present level in 1956, we spent many holidays there, fishing, swimming, and later water skiing. We had a holiday 'shack' on the Howqua arm of Lake Eildon at Macs Cove. Uncle John and Aunty Marj and our cousins John and Jan were part of these holidays as well as family friends and school friends. Boss tried unsuccessfully to focus our activities on fishing alone! Without exception we all enjoyed years of healthy, happy times at Lake Eildon.

Mum and Dad supported us all in our various interests. We were indeed fortunate to experience such a stable family life during those formative years!"

Neil Brock
(Peter's eldest brother)

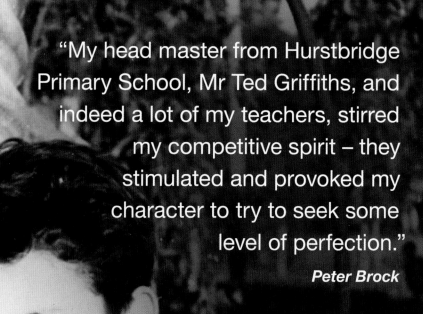

"My head master from Hurstbridge Primary School, Mr Ted Griffiths, and indeed a lot of my teachers, stirred my competitive spirit – they stimulated and provoked my character to try to seek some level of perfection."

Peter Brock

Peter Brock, Anzac Avenue in Hurstbridge.
(Photo supplied by Neil Brock)

Top – Hurstbridge 1961 Demonstration Team. Knox Shield Winners – Region 13 – Lilydale 25 March 1961. Front Row, Peter Brock holding the Winner's Trophy, with brother Neil far right front row. (Photo supplied by Neil Brock)

"I loved footy and played for the Diamond Valley League after having captained the school football team at Eltham High. I even trained with my beloved Collingwood for a while but found I got frustrated when I had given it my all to get the ball down the ground only to have it intercepted because someone else had stuffed up.

At the same time, I was exploring my love of machinery. It was me and my mates out in the chook house at Mum and Dad's place. We got this rocket together, it was a real rocket, and we made it in the old chook house, and every now and again Dad would come out and give us the nod."

Peter Brock

"Peter commenced his schooling at Hurstbridge Primary and then went on to Eltham High School in Eltham Victoria. Peter was a very bright student, but found it difficult to get stimulated by the school environment. He did, however, excel at all things sporting. He starred in athletics at primary school and loved his cricket. Once he was tall enough, football took precedence over other sports. He captained his footy team at Eltham High despite the fact that he was still quite short compared to others his own age. He had been put up a year in primary school because he was so bright, which meant that he was a year younger than his class mates. When he left school and started work at Preston Motors, he took great pride in his ability to remember all of the part numbers and components in the Holden manuals, amazing recall that proved to be a great asset later on."

Beverley Brock

Top – Athletics Team, 1958. (The Mercury – The Magazine of Eltham High School, 1958)

Middle – Swimming Team, 1958. (The Mercury – The Magazine of Eltham High School December, 1958)

Bottom – Fire Brigade Whittelsea Show 1961. (Photo supplied by Neil Brock)

News Press Print. JX1281.

PB's school journal from Eltham High School, charting the emergence of a sporting legend. His classmates signed the back cover, and Peter kept the memento all his life.

Top – Cousin Johnny and Peter.

Middle and bottom – Peter waterskiing and fishing on the Howqua at Eildon. (All Photos supplied by Neil Brock)

"During my early days, my family had a rather rudimentary shack on the Howqua arm of Lake Eildon called Macs Cove. Mum and Dad reckoned that we could live cheaper at the river than anywhere else so we would have six or seven carefree weeks over summer swimming, fishing and generally fooling around, living about as close to nature as we could manage. We were, in retrospect, a rather adventurous group of kids. It was pure bliss.

We couldn't afford the good equipment so we would cobble together the things we wanted. Dad and I got this old drop tank from a WW2 fighter aircraft. We cut it in two and made it into a little boat that was not quite 6 ft long. We rigged up a 12-volt battery to run a windscreen wiper motor connected to a long shaft with a propellor at the end. This was sort of like a rudder as well.

I loved to take this out on my own and just quietly meander around the inlet. We made some skis and a friend who had a shack nearby would let us use their power boat and we learnt to ski pretty well. Eventually we got some proper skis and that made skiing really easy.

It was a great way to spend our holidays."

Peter Brock

Peter, pensive at Eildon. (Photo supplied by Neil Brock)

"I was a real daredevil.

I would take on any dare the kids used to give me but it was cars that really got me as a kid. I remember the first car I ever got.

We were all into the phase of paddock bombs and I was 14 and somehow I ended up getting this old Austin 7 off a guy over in Research not far from home. We went over there and got it on a trailer and dragged it home. I remember getting it off in the back yard and I just couldn't wait to get that old, heavy, antiquated body work off it.

I started heaving and chucking things around and I ended up getting it off. I cut away the metal on the bolts with Mum's axe. Now I know we are talking about a wood axe here but the metal was old and rusty and sheared pretty easy, or so I thought.

But I can tell you that forever and a day Mum was not happy with her boy for blunting her good axe because, as you could imagine, in a household like ours, Mum always lit the fire and got the firewood.

Peter leaping with youthful exhuberance.

Opposite top – The Austin 'Paddock Bomb' at Uncle Sandy's *Farm*.

Opposite bottom – Peter at Doreen. (Photos supplied by Neil *Brock*)

"So when it came to getting behind the wheel of a racing car, I took to it like a duck to water."

Peter Brock

Occasionally us boys would get out there and be forced into doing it but just to save any dramas Mum would be out there and splitting the firewood. Dad had a crook back of course which slowed him down a bit.

But certainly when I got the body work off that car, that five-pound Austin 7, as in pounds shillings and pence, it finished up with this bare frame. A bit of angle iron! With the help of John Lovegrove, a mate of mine, we got this thing going. It never had a brake pedal. I never got around to getting a bracket made to actually fit the whole thing up, so it never actually had a brake pedal so I would drive this thing on the gear box.

You might wonder what would happen. Well, you get by! It is a very strange thing which taught me a hell of a lot in life, because I used to have to slip this back to first gear and double the clutch so I learnt to change gears pretty readily, slide it into a bit of a corner and do a bit of a U-turn and switch it off and let it roll to a stop. I'd get out and open a gate or do whatever I had to do. I'd get back in, get the car going and off I went again. It taught me a lot about anticipating, and of course I am talking about driving around a paddock and old tracks. I am not talking about too much driving on the highway. There wasn't that sort of stuff going on.

It was certainly a very interesting experience for a young kid to have to learn to drive a vehicle without that most basic commodity. I did so successfully. There were a lot of ingredients that came into my childhood that made quite a difference as time went by."

Peter Brock

The family farm provided several tracks which helped develop basic handling skills. (Photos by Neil Brock)

Opposite top left – Peter and 'crew' on the farm track.

Opposite top right – A debonair Peter leaning against the family wagon.

Opposite bottom left – Philip, Neil, Lewis, John Lovegrove and Peter studying engine dynamics.

Peter on *a fast* lap of the farm track.

Opposite top – Cousin Johnny, Philip (behind), Peter and Lewis working on the 'Paddock Bomb'.

Opposite bottom – Detail of Peter's Austin 7 engine. (Photos supplied by Neil Brock)

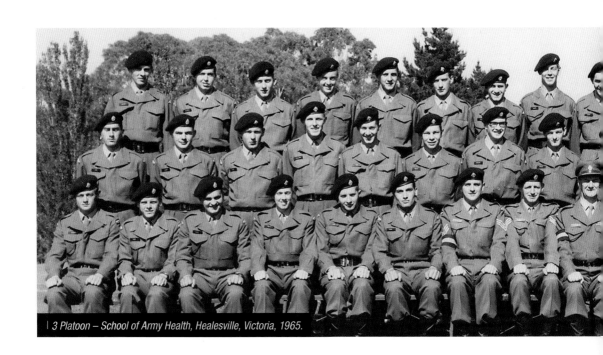

| 3 Platoon – School of Army Health, Healesville, Victoria, 1965.

| National Service Intake Platoon C Company 2 R.T.B. Puckapunyal Victoria.

An evening in the lounge of the Hotel Lennox at Parramatta 1966. Left to right – Johnny La Terra, Joe Corbey, Bruce Howath, Bob Wiese, Merv Longford, Unknown, Peter Turner, Dave Eldridge, Bob Payne, Brian Broderick, Ron Thomas, Peter Brock, Manfred Buckiewicz, Phil 'Speed' Norton, John Meale, David Cecil. All 'Nashos'. (Photo supplied by Peter Turner)

"The national service era

"The national service era was an interesting one for me because I was plucked right out of being a kid, having fun in life with all my mates, car racing and the like. All of a sudden someone threw this National Service business out there. The undercurrent was that this was pretty exciting because none of us knew where to go, what we were doing, what we were in for, and as a 20-year-old that was pretty interesting. It certainly put my motor racing career on hold for a couple of years. I did my basic training at Kapooka and then I got inveigled into the Medical Corp. I didn't know a thing about the human body but a part of it was learning physiology and how the human body works. I kept equating that to how cars worked of course, but I picked it up pretty good. In fact, having come from a scholastic background where I really had no interest or incentive whatsoever, all of a sudden I found myself in National Service doing medical-corp training and I came third in a class of 100 people for physiology. Amongst those were some kids who were studying medicine and had put their study on hold to get their National Service out of the way, so there were some pretty bright kids. I was surprised and impressed with myself that I had taken to this so well.

I ended up running the aid post at Kapooka, which was one of the main recruitment centres at the time. Puckapunyal was the other. I certainly learned a lot of different skills in the army and got to move around the country quite a lot. Fortunately, I didn't end up in Vietnam, I don't believe any of our first intake got there.

It was at Kapooka that I met quite a few celebrities. One of them was the cricketer, Dougie Walters. There were a few rock stars as well. Normie Rowe was at Kapooka too. I guess we were pretty outrageous in some ways and found ways around a lot of the regulations. It helped to be in the medical post. We set up some pretty wild rules for driving the ambulances around the base, and had one set of rules for the guys that got called up as distinct from those who volunteered.

I had a mate there who had contacts in the used car trade, and with his help we managed to get the Austin A30 started, so when we got out things were all systems go to launch my career into motor racing."

Peter Brock

CHAPTER TWO

THE MAN OUTSIDE RACING

"She instilled in me a sense of compassion and concern for others, which I didn't have as a young man."

"As a young teenager, Peter was somewhat shy

around the 'fairer sex'. He did however, make up for that shortcoming in later life!

Being a fit, good looking and charismatic lad certainly gave him the edge with girls and he grew to relish this situation. Whilst still a teenager, his male friends were a couple of years older than him and this gave him access to a wider circle of girls than most boys his age. He never had any trouble 'pulling the chicks'.

In 1964, at the age of 19, he met a decidedly attractive, intelligent and beautifully natured young woman, Heather Russell. Heather shared a love of the outdoors and cars, plus she was not demanding and had a great sense of humour. As they became closer, so did their families and this fact was to strongly influence the path their relationship took as time passed.

Peter and Heather when they started dating, and cutting the cake at their wedding. (Photos supplied by Neil Brock)

Opposite – (bottom) Peter and Michelle Downes on the announcement of their engagement, and (top), Bev and Peter celebrating, among other things, Peter's recent victory at Bathurst.

Peter was conscripted in the first intake of National Service and his time away from Heather only caused the relationship to intensify. It also allowed them both to mature separately. He was fortunate in that Heather shared his love of motor sport and was later to develop a career in racing in her own right.

They became engaged without much fanfare. There was no romantic proposal as such. As it was, their parents sort of took over managing their future and arranged the wedding and the young couple went along with the proceedings.

Unfortunately, the relationship wasn't to be. Peter was single-minded when it came to his new career in motor sport. He was intense and focused, but also became his own harshest critic.

Following his divorce from Heather, there were a number of women who took Peter's fancy. While motor racing took most of his time and energy, there were an interesting array of young women who also took an interest in his need for speed. The fact that they shared this passion was an added advantage.

Several years later Peter met 1973 Miss Australia pageant winner and Channel Seven weather presenter Michelle Downes. They married in April 1974 but this marriage was to be even shorter than his first, ending after only one year. Following their break-up he remained gallant in the extreme and rarely discussed Michelle or any of the traumatic experiences that seemingly filled their lives. Tales from family members on both sides indicated clearly that this was a difficult relationship that was never going to last. On the couple of occasions Peter did open up, it was obvious that despite his being truly in love, it was too difficult to make it work.

Peter and I met at a time when he was hurting and vulnerable and in need of a sound friendship. I was experiencing a difficult time in my own marriage and understood what he was dealing with. The fact that I had no contact with or interest in the media gave Peter a sense of security because he knew that whatever he said would go no further.

Eventually my marriage failed. By this time Jamie was 6 months old. Peter had earlier agreed to become the godfather as Jamie's dad and he were friends. When I mentioned to Ruth at a race meeting that I could no longer work at saving my marriage, Peter opened up about his own feelings. Impressed by his integrity in how he conducted himself I saw in him a sensitive and insecure character that others close to him failed to see.

I had gone to Western Australia to visit a friend and escape for some normality in life just after Christmas of 1976. Peter and his close mate Spear decided to make a surprise visit which was to prove a turning point in both our lives. As a result, I made the momentous decision to leave Sydney and move to Melbourne to be with Peter. Needless to say, we faced the curiosity of both family and friends on both sides. Peter's friends could not see him becoming an instant father and took bets as to how long the relationship would stand the strain."

Beverley Brock

"The 1970s and '80s were trying times

in some aspects of my life and fabulous in others. As you go through life you have these moments of floundering. You go through one relationship after another and there's all this drama in your life. It is very difficult to have a relationship with someone like me who has an all consuming passion.

If you love someone who is right into something, it is most difficult for a partner to understand that, no matter how much they love you.

It occupies every facet of your being, so I was very fortunate in finding Bev, because she understood.

Bev came along and I don't know, I had some sort of innate sense that said: 'This woman is a very good woman and will give you some direction in life.' I thought: 'She's going to give me a sense of steadiness and understanding. She will give you a sense of harmony and balance rather than running from pillar to post and hoping that it

works.' So Bev has made an enormous difference in my life. I credit her and my kids (James, Robert and Alexandra) for bringing a healthy perspective to my life.

She wasn't the woman I held as the ideal woman in my eyes, and I probably wasn't the ideal man in hers. She came from this academic background and here I was this race driver and here's Bev, who is a very attractive but unglamorous sort of woman, different to the women I had known.

She instilled in me a sense of compassion and concern for others, which I didn't have as a young man. I'd crush over anyone to get what I wanted. Bev keeps me sane and the kids keep me grounded. They are full on!"

Peter Brock

| *Above – Peter and Bev.*

"*Not everything was smooth sailing*

throughout the ensuing 28 years we shared. It was in many ways a sound and great relationship. We did, however, know how we felt about each other and what we wanted from our lives. I have a wonderful collection of beautiful letters that Peter wrote throughout those incredible years which left me in no doubt as to the strength of his feelings.

To him there was never a doubt as to how much he loved myself and the kids and that he could not imagine his life without us. We were his stability, his firm foundation which made everything else in his life possible. We shared a fantastic journey where we talked long and deep about anything and everything. We worked well together as a team and literally shared our dreams and aspirations. As I said to our kids, it is better to share an amazing relationship that is 90% fantastic than to walk away and miss out on what proved to be an awesome life.

In the end, our partnership came to an end. He was experiencing a belated mid-life crisis brought on by the horror of the thought of retirement. He was questioning his self worth. He felt like a commodity and needed to start taking charge of his own life and to take responsibility for his own mistakes. He had for many years relied on managers, personal assistants and myself to manage nearly every aspect of his life.

Julie and her family had been closely involved with our family for many years despite the occasional ups and downs. We had once shared some similar beliefs in life but came from entirely differing perspectives in others. Despite emphatic insistence from Peter that Julie was not behind the reason for the separation, he knew he was not living by the principles that he espoused to his kids. I had always loved him enough to want to see him happy, and knew it was time for him to start his new life where he could do as he wished and to handle the consequences without someone else being there to smooth the way.

Some say that those last 14 months of his life were filled with joy and contentment. His immediate family saw a slightly different perspective. What Peter conveyed to his family at that time clearly indicated that it was not quite what he had expected life to be. Maybe he was simply trying not to hurt anyone any more...

No matter what, life takes its own twists and turns and as he always said, 'you create your own reality', so it was as he created it to be.

Would his life have been smoother sailing without his love of women... I doubt it. He certainly lived a full and exciting life, capitalising on every opportunity and 'making the most of every moment'. From my personal perspective, there was very little that I would have wanted to change. To share 28 years with a gentle, sensitive man who wanted to make everything right in the world was a gift. He was creative, driven and cared deeply for people no matter what their origins or beliefs. He was totally committed to making the world a better place. The fact that motor racing gave him his launch pad to make many things possible was irrelevant to who he was as an individual.

Beverley Brock

"It is my family that keeps me sane. Bev provides that sound base. My kids are full on and keep me grounded."

Peter Brock

THE FAMILY MAN

"Not long after Jamie's birth we had visited Melbourne for the Sandown 500. On leaving the track to go home, Peter asked if he could nurse our young bub in the back of the car. He gazed in awe at Jamie, and said: 'This is the closest I will ever come to have a child of my own.'

At that stage of his life, having recently divorced from Michelle, he could not imagine a time when he would be interested in settling down, let alone embracing family life.

When my marriage finally broke down, I told Peter's parents that I had finally given up trying to make it work. Peter then admitted his feelings to me. I was absolutely surprised and had to give deep consideration to what life would be like were I to make the move that he was suggesting. It meant leaving Sydney for a life with him in Melbourne. We had discussed the full implications of such a move. Both of us were wary of marriage having given it a good go but failed miserably, so we made a joint decision that we would not get married but would commit to each other as a couple and family. I had known Peter long enough to know that life as he had known it would not simply cease to exist and that there would be some trying times for both of us for very different reasons.

When Peter and I got together at the start of 1977, Peter became an instant father. He had been through a few tough years and was ready to embrace change.

Peter believed that life with me would give him the stability that he needed and he had little hesitation in diving in to the most radical change of his life to date. He had been sharing his home with his mate, Grant Steers, and Grant was employed at Holden which worked well for all concerned.

Peter splashing Jamie, with Grant Steers watching on in Middle Park.

Opposite – Peter with Jamie.

Peter was remarkable in the way he adjusted to 'fatherhood' given his lack of experience with children.

The home we were renting was one of a pair and the other side came up for sale shortly after we had moved in. Both Peter and Grant were ready to get into the property market but neither was financial enough to go it alone. Peter had come out of his marriage to Michelle without any money and I had only a little from my superannuation account. We bought and moved in next door and instantly set about renovating and gardening. Peter would fail to recognise that others liked to sleep at night and would not stop working until the residents in the other half of the pair would bash on the adjoining wall and yell for him to cease and desist. The garden grew well as he discovered his green thumb and his ability to collect plants from strange locations where they cost him nothing!

Jamie was growing, I was studying, and Peter was exploring business opportunities. We regularly went fishing in his newly acquired 'tinny' and life was relatively smooth sailing.

Peter was racing with the then Holden Dealer Team under the management of John Sheppard and was doing well. He was, however, wanting to have a more hands-on role in running the team as his ideas were often very different to Sheppo's. John taught him much about detail and running a tight workshop but Holden Dealers were sensing that there were opportunities around that would enhance the road-car marketplace and knew Peter was the ideal front man.

Peter and Sheppo had crossed swords and a tacit agreement had been reached whereby if Peter was to come up with a certain amount of money by a certain date, then Sheppo would hand over the reigns to Peter. John felt fairly sure of his position as he knew we had no funds to invest in anything. Not long before Peter had gone to race in England with cardboard folded up inside his shoes to cover the holes so that water wouldn't get in!

An arrangement was worked out with a Holden Dealer from South Australia, Vin Keane, who put up the money to make the move possible. With great delight, Peter walked in to John's office at the deadline and put the money on the desk. John honoured his undertaking and packed up his desk and walked out the door. Peter was now the proud owner of the Holden Dealer Team, albeit in name only.

This started the most exciting, rapidly expanding and developing new motoring business that Australia had seen. It was cutting edge and incredibly successful, so much so that the loan was quickly repaid. In fact it grew so fast that we were forced to move premises four times in the next few years.

While all of this was developing, there was a great deal of intense activity and tension in our household such were the stakes. Then I discovered I was pregnant. I knew that Peter already had more on his plate than he could readily handle and so I kept the news to myself for some months while waiting for the right time. I was fortunate enough not to experience morning sickness nor did I put on weight.

About half way through the pregnancy, I began to have trouble with my spine as I had suffered a broken neck and spinal damage some years earlier. At Peter's suggestion, we went to visit Rudi Webster, a friend who just happened to be the doctor for the visiting West Indies cricket team. Rudi recommended I get an x-ray so it became necessary to spill the beans. To my amazement Peter was ecstatic. He was to become a father in his own right, although he had always thought of Jamie as his own.

As my pregnancy progressed, Peter would declare that it was the longest pregnancy in history despite the fact that he had only been aware of it for half the usual time. He was excited. He thought the time had come for us to move into a home on our own and Grant was ready to invest in his own establishment too. They were really growing up!

After much searching, we bought a period home in Brighton Beach and being the naive buyers we were, we failed to get a building inspection done. We moved in just before Robert was born to find an infestation of white ants. Immediate major renovations were needed and Peter saw fit to build himself extensive aviaries to house his growing interest in breeding finches and budgerigars.

Peter was present for Robert's birth seeing that by some miracle I managed to time the delivery between races. He was so moved by the experience and it was incredible to see this supposedly insensitive man become a soft and doting father. He proved himself to be a devoted father who somehow fitted fatherhood in with his motor racing, his involvement with the Collingwood Football Club, plus his rapidly expanding Special Vehicles business and a great deal of travel. I was, fortunately for him, quite an independent person who was used to managing on my own.

Left to right – Peter and Alexandra; Jamie in Peter's Holden Dealer Team race gear; Peter with Robert on the day of his birth; Peter, Jamie, Ruth and Robert at Robert's 1st birthday.

just disappear. Were it not for the watchful eyes of our wonderful neighbours, he would have fallen victim to either of those traps.

Peter sent me out one Saturday to purchase another home while he went to the football. He wanted to be closer to where he had been raised as a child. The call of open spaces was strong and as I had been raised in similar surroundings on the other side of Australia, I had no objections at all to moving on to a larger property.

By the time the move had been made, Alexandra had arrived. I had gone into labour on the Friday night prior to the Sandown 500. Our lives seemed to revolve around race meetings. My labour had ceased completely at around 9pm and PB had returned home. On his way to practice the next morning he dropped into the hospital to check on how things were proceeding and managed to walk into the delivery room as her head was crowning. 'Boy's head, Bevo!', he said knowing that I desperately wanted a girl for support in a testosterone-driven household!

What time he got at home was devoted to playing with the kids. He was in fact simply a larger version of them and just as much of a handful. Robert proved himself to be a miniature version of his father at a similar age. Ruth, Peter's mum, would often express surprise at just how many things Robert did that his father had done at the same age that his brothers hadn't.

The media got word of Robert's birth and I was given the chance of agreeing to a family interview for a woman's magazine. Should I have chosen not to, then there was to be an article appear in 'Truth' instead. The choice was simple and there began my relationship with the media. My life was to change forever.

Robert proved to be such a handful and we soon realised we needed to move away from the attraction of the rail line and the beach. He could scale a 6-foot fence before he was two and would

He delivered his darling daughter following a Leboyer birth, gave her a bath and instantly left for the track. We had agreed that he could name the boys and I the girls, but that agreement must have gotten lost in the excitement. On arrival at Sandown, he won pole position and in the resulting interview announced to the world on TV that he had just delivered his daughter Alexandra! The first I knew of the choice of name was a nurse coming into my room and asking me if she could nurse Alexandra. She had seen the interview on the news. I was somewhat confused as I didn't know any names had even been discussed. The dye was cast and the name was set in concrete, irrespective of any previous agreements. Who was I to argue?

We once again moved to our new home in leafy Eltham when Alexandra was 3 months old. At that stage Peter was racing in the International Series for Touring Cars as well as the Australian Touring Car Championship and out of the first 11 weeks in a huge home with an acre of garden he managed just 14 days at home. I had a baby and two demanding young boys plus a home and garden to manage. When Peter would finally arrive home he would expect our world to stop so we could make the most of the moments he had with us. I would find them all hiding in cupboards or out in the garden, but as soon as there was trouble the kids came to me. Peter was hurt by this reaction as he felt they should go to him. Once I explained that in order for that to happen he needed to be home a bit more so they really got to know him, he came to understand that something needed to change.

It was about this time that things started to go downhill with Holden. We had built a self-contained apartment adjoining our home for Peter's mum and dad as his mum's health was failing. We wanted to look after them. To Peter, it was his way of repaying them for all they had given up to support him through his life.

We struggled through the emotional turmoil the split with Holden caused and the subsequent loss of his Special Vehicles business. Many could not understand the personal pain that loss caused Peter. He had loved the opportunity to create amazing road cars. He loved the designing aspect plus the engineering to develop a road car that outperformed all others on the road. It was as though a part of him had been amputated.

All this was occurring while the children were growing and developing as miniature human beings, as Peter often put it. He wanted to shape their attitudes and to be the perfect role model."

Beverley Brock

Opposite – Peter as the family man. (New Idea, 14/03/1981 – Picture Greg Noakes)

Top – Robert, Jamie, Peter and Alexandra.

Middle – James, Peter and Robert at Rob's 2nd Birthday.

Bottom – Peter and Alexandra. (New Idea, 14/03/1981 – Picture Greg Noakes)

Top left – Peter gardening at Eltham, with the 'assistance' of Rob and Alex.

Top right – Peter with Rob.

Middle right – Peter and 'DD' (darling daughter) in the kitchen at Eltham.

Bottom right – Peter with Rob and Alex in school uniforms.

Peter with the boys in the pits at Waneroo (now Barbagarllo) in WA, taken for a WA newspaper.

Clockwise from top left – Alexandra and Peter in the garage at Bathurst; family shot at test drive day at Calder in 1986; Alexandra and Peter in the pits at Bathurst during driver rest in 1997, just as the car was showing engine troubles whilst leading the race; a family pic at Eltham for an article in New Idea (photo by Greg Noakes); and Peter hugging Alexandra in the garage at home.

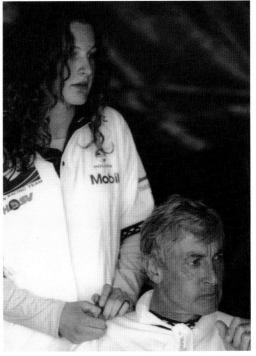

Clockwise from top – Peter and Alexandra look on while Robert checks out a kid's Suzuki farm bike; Robert, Alexandra (borrowing Rob's Mortar) and Peter at Rob's Graduation Day; and Peter with the kids at the airport.

Robert and Peter at the Grand Prix Rally.

'What's it like to have Peter Brock as a father?'

is one of the first things I'm asked when people find out who my father is, although these days it would be more past tense. Everyone except for one person has been surprised by the answer, which has always been, 'I've never known anything else, so I don't have any other experience to compare it to. He was always just my dad.' That being said, I have to admit that I've had opportunities to do things that not many others would have, and at my age I can appreciate the unique experiences that I've had compared to others.

Because the race at Bathurst is almost a religion in itself, the annual pilgrimage was common to a few families. Because a race team has to be at the track days before the race, James, Alexandra and I would be excused from school if holidays hadn't started yet, pack up in the car and off we'd go on an annual drive. Back when the Bathurst Easter Enduro was on, Alexandra and I were roused well

before the sun was up to wish Dad luck and then we'd drift back off. If we were lucky, we'd wake up in time to catch the start of the race. The early hours of the morning of that race were magical. The glowing disc brakes were mesmerising, not to mention the smells from the various corporate tents that were around the track side as they prepared breakfast for the visitors. Back then, Alexandra and I were able to wander into most on the back of our names alone and have a small plate if the catering staff were generous.

Relaxing as a family wasn't very common because of Dad's hectic life. So getting away on a round-the-world trip as a family was a memorable experience. Admittedly, I spent a fair bit of my time through Europe with my nose in a book. Now don't get me wrong, it's not that I wasn't excited about where I was, there was just so much snow covered landscape that I could watch go by with curiosity.

Top – Family shot sitting on the stairs at Nutfield.

Below – Peter and his grandson, Oliver. (Alexandra Summers personal collection)

After Dad's first retirement from the V8s he invited me to navigate for him in the Grand Prix Rally. No one in their right mind would say no to that. How could they? It was exciting, and also a great one-on-one bonding experience. Dad and I had never really had that kind of thing before. He never had the time, but it was fun. Spending a week on the road trying to get from one point to another with some cryptic clues to make sure we approached our destination from the right direction was interesting, especially when trying to do it on the fly at 80kms an hour, with some of the other competitors coming from other directions making it really confusing.

These are just some of the most memorable times of having my father. Sharing him with Australia was part of life, and because of it I had some great experiences to offset the fact that having family time with Dad was a rarity. And I wouldn't change a moment of it."

Robert Brock

(Peter's son)

A teenager Peter driving the machinery, with his dad on the family farm in Doreen.

Opposite – Peter in the shed on the farm, Peter advertised for Tri Steel Sheds and made sure he 'test drove' the product.

"I was born in this district, at Hurstbridge, just down the road. I was raised on this farm. I learned to drive on this farm. I learned to drive at the age of seven in an old Chev truck. It all happened on the flats down at the bottom of the hill. You might be interested to know that this farm has been in the Brock family since 1860. My family cleared the land and now I am putting all the trees back again. Which I think is a delightful paradox."

Peter Brock

"Peter's early childhood was spent in the sleepy hollow of Hurstbridge

but whenever possible he would spend time with his aunt and uncle on Kirkliston, the family farm in Doreen. What he loved most was the freedom it gave him to be outdoors and to be able to play with the farm machinery. He also revelled in the fact that here he was, an only child spending time with very special relatives who had no children of their own. He wasn't having to compete with his siblings for his parents' attention and found that he was given more freedom than at home and could indulge in his passion for mechanical things that moved.

So, as he saw his own children reaching the age where space and nature had huge advantages, it was natural that life on the farm beckoned. On a rare Sunday off, the family went driving and visited the farm just one property away from his paternal grandparents' property. This was where his mother had grown up. By coincidence it was for sale. It certainly looked interesting but when the discussion

came up with his parents and aunt and uncle, it was decided that it would be a better option to purchase the family farm off the Brock estate.

That would mean that the farm would stay in the family's hands and there would be money for the two aunts and two uncles who were aging, held a share and needed money for their retirement. Uncle Sandy and Aunty Norma still farmed their own plot on the adjoining farm and were running cattle on the original property. They were still going to be able to do that under this proposed arrangement so everyone was happy.

Peter was by now an avid environmentalist and so looked forward to planning how to make the most of the haven he wanted to create for himself and his family. It was unfortunately about this time that the wheels fell off his relationship with Holden and major change was to take place in his life.

By the time that scenario had eventuated, the land had been purchased and plans for the home were well under way so there was no turning back. It just meant that the funds that were once there disappeared into a black hole that was keeping the Special Vehicles business

going. Peter was not to be daunted. He threw himself into the development of the property with such vigour that the kids were left standing.

We had chosen to have Alistair Knox, known as the 'father of mud brick dwellings' design the home as we had been living in one of his homes in Eltham. Alistair had designed a self-contained dwelling for Peter's parents to live with us, as Peter's mum's health was declining. Alistair had gone out and inspected the farm to decide where it was best to place the imposing mud brick home that we had jointly designed. On one such trip, I had taken Alistair out to the farm and had driven across a flooded creek to a far-flung hillside to check out the suitability of a location we liked. Alistair was not a well man and prone to asthma attacks. On the way back over the gravel creek crossing the car became bogged and Alistair's breathing started to suffer as his stress levels rose. I was scared stiff that I was killing him and had no way of getting him help.

We eventually made it back to safety and changed our minds as to the location of the home. Plans were drawn up to suit the new site and the decision made for Alistair's son Hamish to build his father's creation for us. It was something completely different to anything he had designed before and he was excited about the new direction he was headed.

Unfortunately, Alistair never got to see his grand design come to fruition. It took a concerted effort for us to make sure that Hamish built the house as his father had envisioned instead of out of concrete blocks and steel that were Hamish's preferred materials at the time. Mud brick was our dream and to make the bricks out of the clay on our own property was the intention. The only thing that didn't come to pass was the ox blood floor that Alistair had wanted us to have in the entrance foyer. It seemed that the technique for this innovation had been lost in the annals of time and passed with Alistair's death.

Above – Peter testing out the pool.

Opposite – Development at Kiah Kerrabee with (top to bottom) Peter's mum Ruth watching on; Peter with Alexandra and Robert; and Peter assisting in the pool construction.

The 'studio' that was to be Ruth and Geoff's home was completed first as it was important that they be moved and settled as soon as possible. Brock males are renowned collectors of 'stuff' and it was a major undertaking to transfer years of accumulated goodies back to the property he had originally grown up on. Our family moved into the partially completed main dwelling in the depths of winter when mud and sludge were abundant. There were few windows in situ, no doors, one semi completed bathroom and a bare kitchen area, but the enormous fireplace and hearth were operational. We placed a caravan at the back door so we had a kitchen of sorts to feed the family. Take aways were not part of the health regime in our family.

In essence, we were camping in a construction site, but such was Peter's excitement at moving in to his new creation that there was no consideration of doing it any other way. Over the next two years, the home grew to completion around us. We planted over 10,000 native trees and bushes, which he was determined would be done as a family activity. He couldn't understand why the kids didn't quite share his enthusiasm for life on

the land. Our kids were new to this side of life and would escape from the farm work whenever possible. However, whenever the opportunity arose, Peter could be seen ferrying the kids and their friends around the farm in the bucket of his tractor or piled into the trailer behind the Maverick when heading off to another bonfire or wood collection mission. They had picnics down by the creek and collected mushrooms, anything to enjoy the outdoor space we were establishing.

We considered the builders and tradesmen a part of our family as they were with us for so long. Hamish and Peter were kindred souls whose minds saw 'possibilities' that others missed. The fact that there was little money to spend on these fantasies meant nothing to either visionary. When I would decry the lack of funds for yet another 'must have', it was simply:

"Bevo, you can talk the bank manager into anything...Don't be negative, let's just bite off more than we can chew and then chew like hell!!!!"

And so the massive project rumbled on. Buildings kept growing, sheds kept appearing and machinery kept filling them. Organic orchards with fruit trees of every imaginable kind were planted and equally organic vegetable gardens grew in size. These all had to be fenced and netted to protect them from the deer and birds. Ponds appeared to both beautify and catch the run-off

from the massive roof. Native and gold fish were brought to fill the numerous ponds and dams. A swimming pool was put in to make sure that the kids didn't have to go elsewhere for summer entertainment and their friends could come and stay in the enormous rumpus room.

One of the orchards became the home for the chooks and another of approximately one third of an acre became the home for the beautiful finches to breed to their hearts' content. Peter would retreat there to quietly regroup his thoughts or to upgrade the nesting sites. The maintenance of the orchards that housed his birds was left to others with a more pragmatic approach to farm life.

Peter thrived on this massive undertaking and spent every available waking moment creating his haven now that he was no longer able to build his cars. He had re-established a good working relationship with Holden but his contract always stipulated that he could not return to the one thing he loved most. Holden had now established their own special vehicles operation in conjunction with Tom Walkinshaw. They were

now in charge and wanted no competition or interference from Peter.

Peter threw himself into eastern philosophy and made sure he taught his kids all of the elements of living a calm and peaceful life; one where you could create your own reality. He had become a dedicated environmentalist and was employing sustainable living methods. We were organic and vegan and, wherever possible, self-sufficient. Our kids raise their eyebrows these days when they are reminded of some of the more adventurous methods we employed at home. At one stage we had them hand-grinding our home grown organic wheat into flour so we could make our own pasta!!!!

No matter what went on in the outside world, at home on the farm we lived quite an idyllic existence. We had started the Peter Brock Foundation following his retirement and frequently had groups of people doing courses at home. We inevitably had kids who were doing it tough living with us, and the dinner table was rich with deep philosophical discussions. There was never a time that Peter could come home and be content to just sit and appreciate what he had created. There was always more to be done to complete the space that gave him the ability to refresh his body and soul. Peter was so determined to spend as little time as possible away from the family and property that he would often fly home after an interstate function and return the next day to complete his commitments.

In hindsight, we probably turned our kids off many aspects of our chosen lifestyle, but Peter managed to instill in them a sense of self, an ability to rise above the expectations of others and to always do what is right by the world around them being as it is the only one we have got. As a result our children have grown up to be fine, intelligent young adults that I am very proud to call my own. As parents we learn by our mistakes and whilst I am sure we made plenty, our children have survived to be capable parents themselves who must now go through the journey of discovery that parenting is the hardest job any of us will ever undertake.

Peter knew that for much of our lives his focus was on his sport or his business, which meant he wasn't there for his family as much as he would have liked. The benefit of hindsight is powerful but that is the way of life. We cannot change what is, and why would we want to in our situation anyway? We shared so many wonderful experiences, met amazing people and journeyed to incredible places. We had a life few would ever experience and whilst it was often trying and demanding, it was both exhilarating and unique."

Beverley Brock

Top – Family Shot on the steps at Kiah Kerrabee; the view looking down the newly planted fenceline; a little older but another family shot in the walkway.

Opposite page – The view from the main house to Ruth and Geoff's round house across the newly constructed ponds.

MEDITATION PERGOLA

KIDS' WING

WORKSHOP AND CARPORT

MAIN HOME

GEOFF'S ORCHARD AND CHOOKS

GEOFF AND RUTH'S HOME

WORKSHOP

An aerial view of the family farm at Kiah Kerrabee.

NEW ORCHARD

FARM HELPERS' COTTAGE

ORCHARD AND FINCH BREEDING

ORCHARD AND CHOOKS

1ST SHIPPING CONTAINER

CATERPILLAR

2ND SHIPPING CONTAINER

RACE TEAM

"Peter's mum, Ruth, grew up on a property one farm removed from his dad Geoff's property. But they attended different schools and rarely crossed paths as children. Ruth and Geoff really met as young adults when Geoff would ride his horse across to call on the young, attractive and athletic Ruth. They married in August 1940 and set up home in the local district, eventually living in the Hurstbridge township and later built a home in Wattle Glen, just down the road.

Ruth was a talented tennis player and played locally and the occasional interstate game while raising their four lively young sons. Geoff was a man of many talents. In those days he was known to have something of a Heath Robinson capability. He at one time operated the local garage as he was an accomplished mechanic, but he also became skilled at the emerging electronics industry and for a number of years was in demand to install televisions and to repair radios. He found that

Peter was a most handy child to have around as he would scramble up onto roofs and up trees and poles to find the best possible location and direction for the aerial. To Peter this meant gaining praise for his daredevil approach to heights and his willingness to take on any task his dad gave him.

Peter and his father went into a partnership in what became the Diamond Valley Speed Shop which did much to help Peter get established in motor racing. It did not flourish as a business, however, and eventually went under. Geoff went into real estate and property management after the demise of the Speed Shop. Peter always remembered what his parents sacrificed for his career and as soon as he was able did all he could to repay them for their unswerving support.

Beverley Brock

Opposite page – Geoff and Ruth Brock's wedding, 1940.
(Photo supplied by Neil Brock)

Top – Geoff working at Diamond Valley workshop.

Below left & right – Geoff and Ruth.
(Photos supplied by Neil Brock)

"Mum was a very competitive
person, she was an excellent
sportswoman, a Victorian
tennis champion."

Peter Brock

Top – Peter, Ruth and Geoff at the launch of the Director.

Above – Ruth and Geoff at Peter's surprise 40th.

Right – Geoff and Ruth Brock at Peter's wedding to Michelle Downes.(Photo supplied by Neil Brock)

Opposite page – Peter and Ruth at their house on Meadow Creek Road.(Photo supplied by Neil Brock)

Top – Ruth, Geoff, Peter, Aunty Marg and Uncle John at Bathurst.

Right – The four brothers at the Brock family reunion at Kiah Kerrabee, 2001.

Below – Neil, Peter and Lewis.

Opposite top left – Uncle Sandy, Bev, Alexandra, Geoff and Peter at Geoff's last birthday at Kiah Kerrabee.

Opposite right – Santa Brock.

Opposite bottom – Peter with Uncle Sandy.

"As a child, Peter spent much of his time
with his Auntie Norma and myself on our farm at
Doreen. It was always obvious that whatever he
set his mind to do, he would strive to do it to the
very best of his ability. You could even say he was
a little stubborn in that regard.

His interest in farm life was not in the cows or
sheep but in the tractor and the truck, or in fact,
anything with wheels. He rode his bike as fast as
possible, but when he was allowed to drive the
Grey Fergie tractor he would show good control.
He understood the dangers involved. In later life,
this ability to control a vehicle became evident in
his racing career.

There was another side to Peter even then,
because although he liked to be active, he could
lay on the floor with a pencil and paper and draw
for hours, particularly when it was hot outside.
The drawings were mostly car designs, but in
later life he was to produce some outstanding
works of art.

Football was his favourite sport and we spent
many hours playing kick-to-kick on Sunday
afternoons. I hoped that he would play for
Collingwood one day but his choice to enter
car racing proved to be a good decision."

Uncle Sandy

Enjoying the cool, calm waters in the Daintree River (Port Douglas) with James, Rob and Alexandra.

"During the mid 1980s, when the children were young, the family would high tail it to Port Douglas for school holidays. These were true breaks and Peter would grab the opportunity and join myself and the kids for a few weeks. We had an apartment and then a home in the hills plus a modified inflatable and would head out to Low Isle where it was possible to swim in the ocean. Unless you had a pool, swimming was not an option in summer as the water was full of stingers.

It was not uncommon for Peter to load the family in the little craft and defy weather warnings to leap from wavetop to wavetop as we headed out for the relative calm on the lee side of the island. I would cling to babies and toddlers while we thumped our way across the turbulent waters.

Peter loved the thrill of speed on the ocean as much as he did on the land. Not all of us shared that passion, but it was truly worth it when we reached the beautiful waters protected by the little island. Unfortunately, we would then have to brave the return journey at day's end.

We explored the Daintree and nearly lost Robert when he fell into Mossman Gorge. We are eternally grateful to a man swimming nearby who dove deep into the waters to fish him out after being swept down the overflow of a waterfall. We drove our trusty HK station wagon through rainforests and tablelands to take in as much of the countryside as possible."

Beverley Brock

Left – Peter, Rob and James on Low Isles off Port Douglas.

Above right – Peter and the kids in New Zealand.

Right – Peter and Alexandra on the beach in Port Douglas.

Peter on the Frans Josef Glacier in New Zealand.

Peter and the kids experiencing the thrill of jet boating in New Zealand.

"In the late '80s, when the wheels fell off our lives

with Holden, money was short, our property in Queensland was sold to keep things afloat at home. From this time on, holidays were fitted in with racing commitments. It became a regular feature to fly to New Zealand just after Christmas where there were a couple of races that Peter was invited to participate in. The kids would come along and in between the two races we would visit Rotorua, Taupo, and drive the rugged mountain roads of the north island at warp speed. The kids might be throwing up in the back, but Dad was never daunted. We jet boated and went into the mountains and to the Bay of Islands. On one occasion we even found time to do the train trip from Queenstown across the South Island to Greymouth and to climb on Franz Joseph Glacier.

So while there were work times that took precedence, holidays could be fitted in and this gave the children a chance to see most of New Zealand where the locals welcomed us as if we were New Zealanders."

Beverley Brock

"During the early '90s the kids were getting older

and James was choosing not to accompany the rest of the family. We were no longer cool! He did, however, still tag along for the regular trips to Bathurst. Here there was very little chance to do anything other than work at the track. There was one rare trip to the Jenolan Caves. Bathurst was strictly work and for many years there were two trips per year, one for the big event, and the other for the 12-hour at Easter. The kids also made it to see Dad's great victory at the 24-hour race towards the end of his illustrious career. Jamie co-drove to victory with his Dad in the ute event which made the whole weekend even more special.

Below – Peter and the kids in the Olgas and (bottom left) Peter resting in the quiet waters at Palm Valley.

Opposite page – Peter and the kids, Standley Chasm.

We were given many amazing opportunities to travel for 'work'. One in 1995 took us to Central Australia when a holiday program on TV wanted to film Peter and his family on whatever Peter decided was his favourite place to visit. He chose Palm Valley in Central Australia as it was a place that held his fascination for many a year. Here was a pristine, ancient valley visited by few that held remnants of vegetation seen only in a couple of places on Earth.

As long as we could cope with a film crew for the first days we could then extend our stay and remain as a family for a few days longer. Jamie was working at this time so the rest of us climbed ancient ranges, explored beautiful hidden valleys and gorges, swam in streams still swollen from recent floods. It was superb and private and gave Rob and Alexandra a glimpse of a seemingly never changing land."

Beverley Brock

"How awesome is our country? How fortunate am I that I get to visit it and become inspired to paint what I see? If only I could do it justice!"

Peter Brock

Alexandra, her girlfriend Genty and Peter at a lookout in Tassie and (below) a rest from playing in the snow at Lake Como in Italy.

"Travelling with Peter Brock:
epic embarrassment and extreme frustration, with a police escort. Travelling with Dad was always adventuresome – from dealing with ABS systems in a rental car through the icy roads of the Swiss/Italian Alps to the armed soldiers advising us to turn around after we were distracted by various well-lit religious buildings in Jerusalem. That night, at a travellers' internet café, the New Zealand owner happily recognised him and stopped to chat.

There are three experiences I believe best describe the infuriating, scarring but mostly joyous experiences of travelling with my dad. And we did a lot of travelling, especially in 1998, when we took a world tour*.

1997 Auckland, New Zealand
Dad filmed a show in New Zealand very similar to his Australian counterpart *Police Camera Action*. (The show, *Police Stop*, featured motorway patrols chasing and apprehending various hoons.) I journeyed to New Zealand with Dad, sans the rest of the family, and whilst there the show wanted to explore the results of law breaking by doing a tour of Auckland Prison. Dad walked around with the Chief Guard, discussing protocol, showing holding cells, mentioning the number of fleas. Not wanting to be in the way I was left BY MYSELF in a hallway, in a jail, opposite occupied cells AT FOURTEEN. When a very angry occupant glared at me for over a minute from his small window, I decided it best to interrupt the shoot by squealing and running to Dad. Later in the trip, we were taken on patrol and surprisingly got involved in a very real high-speed chase on the motorway. The very well-trained policemen used all the force necessary to apprehend a man who clearly did not wish to be apprehended. We sat in the back of the finally motionless police car attempting to work out where the apprehended offender was going to sit: next to me, or Dad.

Newark Airport, America
We often had the delight of having a late flight change, or stopover, or diversion, or I don't know, it was late. For some reason we were commuting from one part of Newark airport to the other. You know those signs on the bottom of escalators that say NO TROLLEYS, in bright yellow, on every escalator, in every airport? Well Dad selectively ignored those and. as predicted, the trolley got wedged in at the end, bags fell, we fell, others fell on the fallen, it was a disaster. I died from emotionally-based embarrassment, amplified by the very angry Hispanic woman yelling at me in Spanish and me quietly pleading, 'It wasn't me, it was HIM.' Dad just laughed.

Vatican City, Italy
When we reached our southernmost point, Rome, I began to fully appreciate my father's driving skills. Rome traffic has little logic. We drove through the city, left down a breathtaking street, right down another. Everything was really old, apparently the police also, as a man stood in front of us after another quirky death defying turn. A man in a tunic, and leggings, with a gun; wait, that's no policeman, that's a Swiss Guard, and this is no street, this is the Vatican! Dad pleads with the man repeating 'Touristo' a dozen times whilst I, again, died in the back seat, as they stopped all traffic to loudly and obviously allow us to turn around to a symphony of horns.

Travelling with Dad was an adventure, he was always willing to try anything, though the speed with which he reached a destination, would see it and move on, often defied one's ability to actually experience anything. But we sure did see some amazing, bizarre and memorable things."

Alexandra Summers
(Peter's daughter)

*Tour may or may not have been based on the awesome assumption that the world would end due to the Y2K bug.

Peter at the Daly Waters Pub in NT, (above) posing with number plates, (below) with staff and (opposite) adding his moniker to the wall.

"These were the gems that made our crazy lifestyle so incredibly memorable. No matter that the kids had to share their dad with the rest of Australia, they also managed to get some rare and wonderful opportunities that few of their mates would ever experience. This more than balanced the books."

Beverley Brock

Clockwise (from top left) – Rob and Alex giving Peter seaweed dreads near Fremantle; at Niagara Falls; camping on Fraser Island; a 'grey nomad' in the Northern Territory; taking a dip at Katherine Gorge; and with Bev at the pyramids in Egypt.

| Bev and Peter enjoying the quad bikes experience on a station in the Northern Teritory.

"In 2003 the only trip on offer for the 'ageing' Peter and myself was to work for the Northern Territory Tourism Commission. It was a trip designed to show the grey nomads that you could take a fantastic trip throughout the entire state in an ordinary car. We were accompanied by three guys who set up daily connections with a mobile satellite dish to keep viewers abreast of our travels.

It was a great success in every way. There was a huge amount of interest and we got to travel the rugged outback, visiting places we had only dreamed of. We flew into Ayers Rock to pick up our vehicles –Holdens of course! – and our camping gear.

There we stayed in the crocodile-shaped resort and then drove off to eventually arrive in Darwin. Along the way we stayed in tents, caravan parks, hotels, resorts and cabins just to show what was available. We visited the Olgas, and the Rock, aboriginal settlements, Katherine Gorge, Alice Springs, Litchfield National Park and, of course, the awesome Kakadu plus many spots in between.

The year before we had camped in Tasmania between Christmas and New Year. We had built a purpose-built camping trailer so that Peter and I could camp our way through the outback in our retirement! Sadly, that was never to eventuate."

Beverley Brock

CHAPTER THREE

THE BROCK HERITAGE

*"I live in the NOW but my heritage
has made me who I am!"*

"The first cars appeared in Australia in 1897 and

because of the tyranny of distance, Australian inventors were forced to produce their own local product in order to take developing technology forward in their own way. In 1903, a rail strike in Melbourne provided Henry James and his mate Charles Kellow the opportunity to find a valuable use for the fledgling automobile industry. They managed to persuade the head of the *Argus* newspapers that they could deliver the papers to country districts in the absence of the trains. True to their word they were able to leave the printers in Melbourne by 3am and drop papers at Kyneton, Castlemaine and then arrive in Bendigo by 9.30am, an hour earlier than the train could manage.

Soon after a group of motor cyclists rode to Tooradin and decided to organise a combined car and motor cycle event. Sydney Day and James Coleman, along with Peter's Great Uncle Henry (Harry) organised for 60 motorists and 30 cyclists to drive to Mordialloc on Sunday Dec 6th. Just a week later saw a group of some 56 keen enthusiasts form the first Auto Club of Victoria. They didn't all own cars but shared a passion for the new technology. By the next month they had more than 100 members.

In 1905 Harry, who was employed by Dunlop, ran the first Reliability Motor Contest from Sydney to Melbourne, a distance of 572 miles and run over many classes of road. There had only been three previous such events in the world. Of the 23 cars entered, 17 finished.

This passion for things mechanical and competitive was taken up by Geoff, Peter's dad, and enthusiastically followed by Peter while still very young. It was to lead to a life at the pinnacle of Australian motor sport and the manufacturing of fine-performance road vehicles."

Beverley Brock

Above – An outing for the early motoring enthusiasts leading to the formation of the RACV. (Documentation and image supplied by Beverley Brock)

Opposite page – Alexander and Elizabeth Brock. (Photos supplied by Neil Brock, digitally merged)

Previous page – The young Henry James (Harry), Peter's Great Uncle.

"The Brock family history has been traced

back to its farming heritage in the Parish of Kirkliston just out of Edinburgh, Scotland in 1631. Peter's eldest and wisest brother, Neil, has spent many years researching this and discovered that seven members of that family emigrated to Tasmania in the 1820s and some, along with their descendants, moved across to the mainland in the ensuing years.

John Brock, one of the original immigrants, and his family successfully managed to bring their livestock across to Port Phillip in what was seen as a particularly hazardous crossing. They moved up what was then known as the Salt Water River, now known as the Maribyrnong, to eventually reach Emu Creek in the Romsey district. Here John established 'Head Station' on the Bullanda Vale run and went on to extend his pastoral leasings further afield. In 1851 the family were forced to move from their original holding at Bullanda Vale when the property was granted to WJT Big Clarke in the restructuring that followed the separation

of NSW and Victoria. The family then moved to an adjacent property so they could remain in the district. Henry, one of John's sons, married Margaret Reid at Hazel Glen, which is now known as Doreen. The Reid family still retain their original family land holdings. Henry and Margaret set up home in Janefield and took up ownership of several other properties in the district.

Another of John's sons married and set up his home at Bolinda Vale in the Romsey area. He unfortunately met an early end at just 32 after his horse rolled on him. Another son, Alexander, who is the immediate relative of Peter's family, travelled back to Scotland to visit his elderly grandfather and the rest of the family who had remained in Scotland. The diary of this trip to the homeland survives to this day. He subsequently married the niece of Big Clarke who had been granted the original family-land holding at Romsey. Alexander and Elizabeth

The plaque to commemorate the Brock family reunion in 2001.

Below – documentation for the original purchase of the family farm.

Opposite top – Alexander Brock (12 May 1823 – 7 December 1871). Arrived in Australia with his parents in 1833. Son of John Brock and Jean Simpson. Elizabeth Clarke (17 January 1833 – 8 April 1922). Married Alexander Brock 1853. (Photos supplied by Neil Brock)

Opposite bottom – Family Coat of Arms. (Photos supplied by Neil Brock)

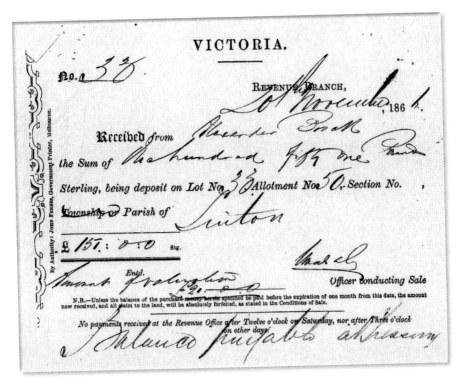

| Brock family reunion 2001.

went on to own extensive holdings in Romsey, Yarck, Shepparton, Avoca, Charlton, Denniliquin, Janefield, Bundoora, Thomastown and the Preston area. The first of their offspring was born at 'Overton' in Bundoora but they went on to build a substantial family home known as 'Oak Hill' in Preston in 1862 where they produced the remainder of their 9 children. This home stayed in the family until 1935.

During this time, Alexander proved to be a leading figure in the community. He became Justice of the Peace and stood for Parliament. In 1866 he bought the 188 acres in Doreen, in the Parish of Linton, County of Evelyn, for the princely sum of 300 pounds and 16 shillings. His son Lewis Clarke Brock took on the ownership at Doreen and passed it on to his son, Lewis Alexander (Boss) Brock, and then to Alexander William (Sandy) Brock. This is the same property that Peter and I bought off the family estate and established Kiah Kerrabee which we held until it became necessary to sell it following our split in 2005.

The property had remained in the family continuously for 140 years which made the sale even more difficult for them all to bear.

The Brock family were a part of the beginnings of white settlement in Victoria and in the ensuing years their descendants have spread far and wide. A reunion at the family farm in Doreen on April 15–16th in 2001 saw 140 relatives come from across the Australian mainland, Tasmania and New Zealand. They ranged in age from two months to their nineties. A plaque to acknowledge the family history was unveiled by local MP and friend, Fran Bailey, at the top of the hill overlooking the property."

Beverley Brock

CHAPTER FOUR

A RACING CAREER
UNEQUALLED

"Motor racing to me, is a competition where I say to myself – 'Let's do this as well as possible with the highest level of skill I have to extract my full potential."

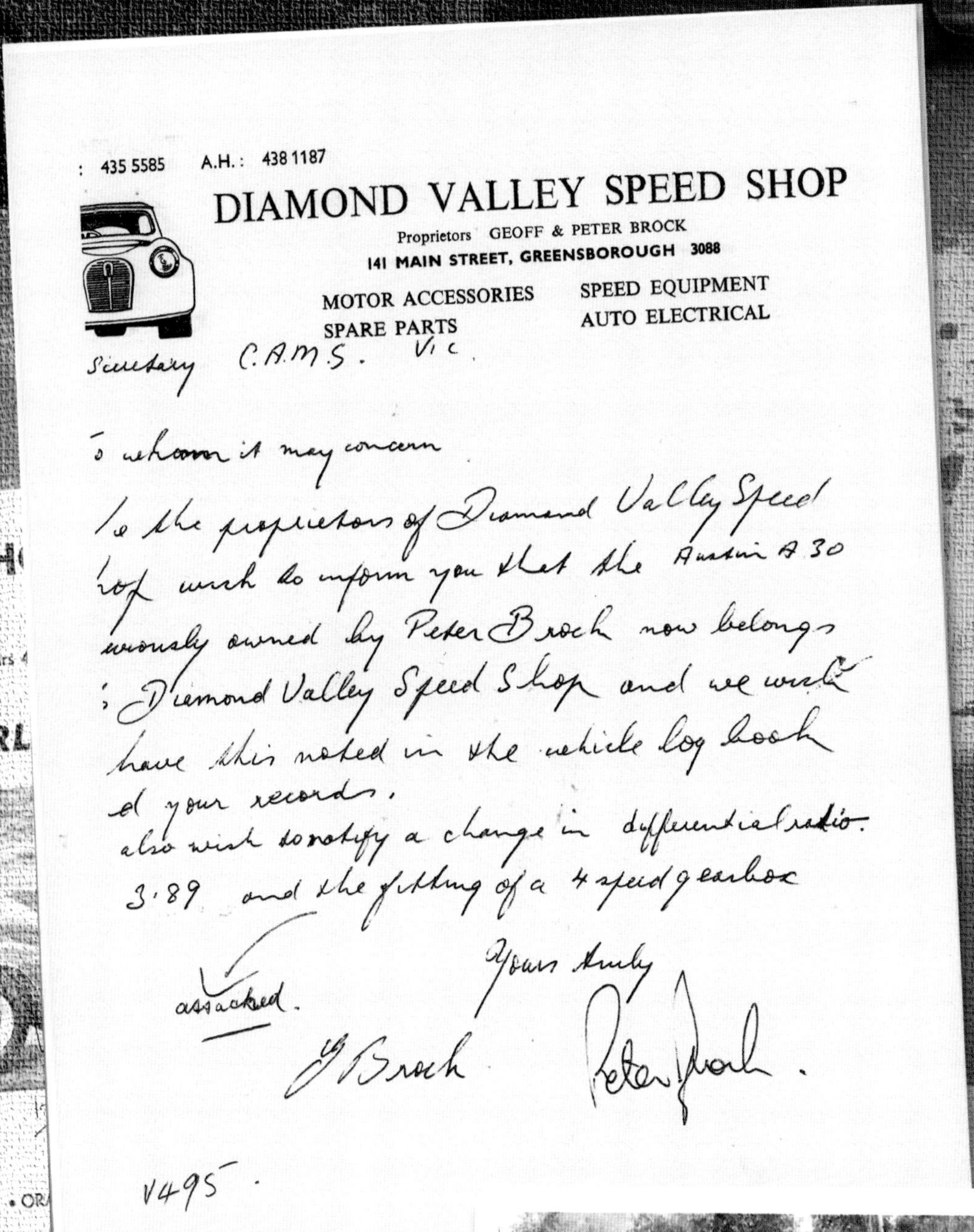

: 435 5585   A.H.: 438 1187

DIAMOND VALLEY SPEED SHOP
Proprietors   GEOFF & PETER BROCK
141 MAIN STREET, GREENSBOROUGH 3088

MOTOR ACCESSORIES   SPEED EQUIPMENT
SPARE PARTS   AUTO ELECTRICAL

Secretary   C.A.M.S.   Vic.

To whom it may concern

We the proprietors of Diamond Valley Speed
Shop wish to inform you that the Austin A30
previously owned by Peter Brock now belongs
to Diamond Valley Speed Shop and we wish
have this noted in the vehicle log book
of your records.

also wish to notify a change in differential ratio.
3.89 and the fitting of a 4 speed gearbox

attacked.

Yours truly

G Brock

Peter Brock.

V495.

Peter's handwritten application for a logbook for the Austin A30
(countersigned by Dad, Geoff, on letterhead from the family business).

Peter Brock's first racing car in action. (Photo from Terry Russell Photography)

Chapter title page – A very young Peter at the beginning of his career with only the family Speed Shop as a sponsor. (Photo from Terry Russell Photography)

Early outing for the rough diamond. (Photo by Terry Russell Photography)

"Peter used his time in National Service to start preparing his first race car. He was running the medical centre and found a ready supply of medicinal alcohol to clean the parts of his motor and gear box.

They worked hard weekends putting this car together. A 179 Holden engine was sourced from a wrecker, an Austin A30 body purchased from Wagga, and parts begged and borrowed from friends.

His dad was there for moral support and served as his first mechanical consultant, but friends such as Ron Bentley, Ken Mitchell and later Terry Hutchinson and John Lovegrove became essential parts of the successful team."

Beverley Brock

The Austin A30 in action. Front row of the grid at Hume Wier. The A30 had been a little refined by now. (Photos from Terry Russell Photography)

"Motor sport has changed considerably.

It has become quite a bit different from what many would think it to be and it's not necessarily the perfect scenario.

There's no point in getting aggravated about the differences between what is and what you would like it to be. In fact, the smart move would seem to be to accept the situation for what it is, change what you reckon are the obvious things you can and make the most of the opportunities presented while always acting with the good of the sport foremost in your mind.

For many years the single most powerful motivating force that drivers, team owners, spectators, sponsors and manufacturers abided by was the love of motor racing. It wasn't all that complicated, really – stories would be told, pictures shown, dreams dreamed and pretty soon those exposed to this, those who felt inclined, would get out there and get organised and have a go.

It would go something like this. Firstly, check out a few mates to find out if they were keen and then, depending on the level of interest, a plan would unfold as to how the race team would be put into action. It just sort of happened and it was always propelled by that deep-seated desire to simply get out there and do it with passion.

So where are we at now, particularly in the world of V8 Supercars, which currently represents the pinnacle of the hopes and desires of the vast motor sport/motor racing audience?

There seems to be a different dynamic in operation. One where the driving force to succeed has changed, not that the people strive harder, are any more committed, but rather that the idea of what it takes to achieve success is now based on different principles.

Motor racing is obviously a very technical undertaking, and as the years have gone on, it has provided participants with a certain aura or image that has enabled those associated with the sport to exploit it to their advantage. I've been subject to and have done this very thing myself, but it is like treading on egg shells. It needs to be done with extreme care and concern since the whole thing can back fire if the motor racing experience is not treated with respect and a level of reverence.

Creating an image or reputation takes more time and effort than most participants have patience for. This current era has a penchant for instant heroes, instant deals and instant success. Anything less is deemed a failure.

Slowly but surely the motivating force has transformed into a force that tends to pay little heed to the love of the sport, it's more likely to be one of expediency.

The 'deal'.

One where the bottom line is money, power and control. Currently egos are going pretty crazy and the atmosphere in the pits resembles some sort of animal mating ritual as these egos go about demonstrating their self importance. Bantam roosters come to mind.

History has little or no significance in the eyes of most of the franchise holders. Even the drivers get caught up in this unfulfilling game where the buck is passed effortlessly to anyone silly enough to have not covered their backsides sufficiently well.

I even heard of a most revered gentleman involved in motor sport being ridiculed because he had the temerity to have an 'old fashioned' stopwatch around his neck. They say those days have gone. Now we have data acquisition. (I thought this was a personal version of just that actually!)

Torana, early HDT drive. (Photo from Terry Russell Photography)

Let's get real!

Franchise holders are worthy of further comment as they are currently having an enormous influence on the direction of this our elite branch of motor sport. It is this very situation that has virtually brought CART to its knees.

During the latter half of the '90s it was decided to grant an entrants' licence to the privileged few who were in the loop at that time. Fair enough. However, others arriving at the V8 scene and wishing to have a go find that the door is closed. They aren't free to join in. They need to do a deal in order to play the game. As a result people get their noses out of joint if the deal doesn't satisfy their idea of how the game ought to be played. There is a lot of petty bickering and arguing and that has an adverse effect on everyone involved. You see when all of the above is the basis of the deal it's extremely rare that it involves anything that is vaguely likely to encompass the love of motor racing or to be primarily for the good of the sport.

While you may argue that this business approach shifts the sport to a new level of professionalism, and there is no doubt that it has many benefits, it also allows many who have no idea of how the sport works to influence the direction and hence the viability and sheer enjoyment that the sport can produce. Who needs the aggro? I certainly don't, and yet that seems to be the aim of many of their quests for money and power.

Of course we need sensible business decisions to be made for the sport I love so much, but we also need to ensure that the passion, the excitement and the unpredictability of this interesting human pursuit are maintained.

There ought to be room for innovation, this is not always in evidence. For instance, set times for pit stops is one idea being floated at this particular point of time and is in my opinion against competition, entertainment and innovation and should be binned immediately. There needs to exist the possibility of choosing, for instance, different tyres, to encourage more manufacturers, more potential outcomes and much more interest.

Finally, let's not forget motor racing is 'dangerous', that's why I chose it. We don't need 'safety cars' to lead the field around in the wet!"

Peter Brock 13TH JANUARY 2003

"You don't have to necessarily win to be successful. You just give it your best shot."

Peter Brock

| *Torana in action.*

A30 Race Results. Winning Races in bold.		
SEASON	POS	CAR
November 26, 1967	DNF	Winton
December 26, 1967	Unplaced	Hume Weir
January 21, 1968	2nd	Calder
January 28, 1968	3rd	Philip Island
April 14, 1968	4th	Hume Weir
May 26, 1968	2nd	Winton
June 9, 1968	2nd	Hume Weir
June 30, 1968	**1st**	**Lakeland**
September 1, 1968	**1st**	**Hume Weir**
September 22, 1968	5th, 5th &4th	Oran Park
November 17, 1968	**1st**	**Templestowe**
December 1, 1968	**1st**	**Winton**
December 26, 1968	**1st**	**Hume Weir**
January 2, 1969	**1st & 2nd**	**Philip Island**
January 26, 1969	**1st**	**Philip Island**
February 16, 1969	**1st**	**Sandown**
March 9, 1969	2nd	Winton
March 16, 1969	**1st**	**Templestowe**
Easter, 1969	**1st**	**Philip Island**
May 18, 1969	**1st**	**Winton**
June 15, 1969	**1st**	**Hume Weir**
September 14, 1969	2nd	Sandown
September 21, 1969	**1st & 2nd**	**Oran Park**
September 28, 1969	**1st**	**Hume Weir**
January 3, 1970	**1st**	**Oran Park**

Peter thrived on the exuberance of motor sport. It gave him a chance to demonstrate his mastery behind the wheel. (Photo by Terry Russell Photography)

An 11-year-old Neil Crompton with *Peter Brock* in 1970. (Photo from Neil Crompton)

"Forty years have passed since I first

crossed paths with Peter Geoffrey Brock. Even re-reading this sentence leaves me shaking my head in disbelief. 40 years... Before I tell a tale, let me back up for a moment.

Motor racing is a unique and rather weird blend of business, show business, sport, engineering, teamwork, personal fitness and human endeavour etc. It is part science, part theatre, part illusion... Peter Brock took up a lofty position in this world. He lived and lived well right at the summit.

Four decades back, as an eager 10-year-old, I devoured the industry bait. Somehow, Peter Brock was able to convey both the competitive joy and Hollywood-style mythology of racing to the extent that my childhood dream and path was cast right there and then and ultimately materialised. Picture Calder Park Raceway on the western outskirts of Melbourne. The year was 1971. The event was called Rallycross. Few of today's V8 Supercar followers would have a clue what this was...

Peter's race car de jour was a concoction of weird bits that started life as a Holden Torana GTR. Not the 'hotter' GTR XU1 that came later. In fact, as I

recall, it was road registered too. Forty years ago I could roll off the rego details. Victorian plate K?? 158 something or other... I dunno.

Early on, it was white with a racy matt black bonnet, which then morphed into a yellow supercharged beast, then later into the car that wore the more familiar red, white and black colours of the Holden Dealer Team.

Sitting alone on the wire fence at the end of the back straight I would stare with a laser focus at this bloke who could command this odd motor car in and out of all kinds of bizarre on-track attitudes like it was a simple play thing. Along the way there was success, trophies, interviews. This was right at the beginning of the Brock brand which was to become a household product for decades to come.

The ritual. Kid watches while hero performs automotive miracles was repeated over and over for many years around the nation. Many will know Peter's driving skills were honed paddock bashing old cars in his youth. Peter excelled in his chosen craft and we all know about his CV...

However, his driving skill is only part of the story. I needed to contribute to my primary school magazine... Year 5 I think it was? Why not 'interview' my favourite racing driver? Peter must have been around 25. No PR machine to craft his act, no marketing managers drumming him about being 'on message'. This was the raw mid-20s Peter Brock. A knockabout bloke from Melbourne's North East who raced a car and smiled a lot. And yes, he answered if you asked. Pretty simple formula really.

A jump into the deep end changed my life... Responding to my nervous, tentative request, Peter willingly engaged. Using my pencil and paper, he took the time to carefully handwrite a full description of a flying lap of Calder Park in the grubby little Torana. It must have taken 15 minutes or more. I still have the tattered piece of paper and the school magazine.

He dutifully answered every single annoying little kid question too, with enthusiasm and passion. I felt like a brother. I was on the inside. This scene was repeated on high rotation throughout his life. But he made me feel special. The interesting thing for me to contemplate today is how he could do this over and over and over and not fade? You either have it or you don't. Peter had it. He had a natural gift and as he began to understand it he used his powers wisely.

What is not understood is that this fan engagement is a double-edged sword. To engage, enthuse, listen, respond and comply is very hard and it takes an enormous mental and physical effort. Before, during and after the racing mission, a driver's mind is totally consumed. How to extract even more from yourself and that machine is a 100%, 24/7 preoccupation.

To later live and work alongside Peter over a long period, I could see that to effectively deliver this sparkle to his army of fans meant giving a tiny little piece of himself away every time...

In equal measure, maybe even the larger part of the sum of Brock was Peter's ability to share the passion and provide an insight in a very Australian way, which made him a unique character. Making you feel as though you were his sole focus, the only fan in the world and transporting you into his world, the special world of the racing driver, was an amazing and rare gift.

Upon reflection, the celebrated life of Peter Brock was as much about his personality and communication as it was his obvious driving skill. Ignore the references 'I' and 'me' in this little yarn. I typically roll my eyes when I read stories filled with 'I' and 'me', but in this instance I wanted to be able to convey a very personal account.

Make no mistake – don't read into this that Peter was a saint. I'm not smitten by the Brock bug, but he holds a very special place in my heart. Saint? Far from it. Like the rest of us he was full of flaws and contradictions, however, he was the master of two universes. For me the measure of the Peter Brock life and legacy is a two-part story. The most obvious is the on-track and related achievements. The record speaks volumes.

In equal measure, though, is Peter's harder to measure contribution to thousands of people who were entertained and came into contact with him. It's what and how he shared that made a big difference. Add this to his racing skill and we ended up witnessing a very special person in action from 1945 to 2006.

If we all had the ability to sit and reflect on our life's work it would be hard to imagine a better legacy than to say we were able to:

Do what we love doing. Do it well. Provide enormous pleasure for many many people. Be the catalyst for others to help them fulfill their ambitions. To simply make people feel good.

Peter Brock did these things and much more."

Neil Crompton
(Professional race-car driver, presenter & commentator)

"Peter Brock was one of the best known and most talented drivers in Australia. He was a great inspiration to all up-and-coming drivers as his skill and his driving record was phenomenal and still stands. His very sad death proved that motor racing is very dangerous for even the best of drivers. It was a tragic blow to Australia and he is sadly missed by all."

Jack Brabham
(Sir John Arthur Brabham – Formula One world champion)

Above left – 3rd August 1957, Jack Brabham, at Brands Hatch, 1957. (Photo – Hulton Archive/Getty Images)

Above right – Peter with Jack Brabham at a Grand Prix dinner.

Opposite – Peter Brock 1971, holding his decanter trophy after winning his Rallycross event.

"If the car is not going fast enough, you have to get yourself going faster first. Others go in to win at any cost."

Peter Brock

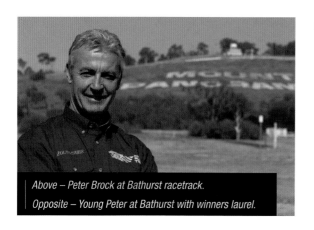

Above – Peter Brock at Bathurst racetrack.
Opposite – Young Peter at Bathurst with winners laurel.

"A long, long time ago on a mountain not so far away, a group of men equipped with picks and shovels, blue singlets, overcoats and a fierce desire for survival and independence, began to fashion a forest drive to the summit and return. They had little budget and only horse drawn power, so by necessity they followed the natural terrain while the property lines governed the general direction.

The result was one of the most difficult and challenging pieces of road that driver's encounter, particularly if you try to achieve maximum speed. The fabled Mount Panorama at Bathurst was born, it became a racetrack years later and was only sealed mid last century and then further developed as time and finances permitted. The position that 'the Mountain' has taken in Australian folklore is now that of 'icon status', and that is not to use the term lightly.

Since I was a very young kid drivers have been embarking upon a quest, a quest to find the 'holy grail' of Australian motor sport. To conquer the fears and myths surrounding the Mountain and all that it represents. Things happen at Bathurst that don't necessarily bear much resemblance to logic, or what is otherwise fair play and reason. It has a peculiar attraction. Some say it is like playing cricket at Lord's, or hearing the crowd roar at the MCG. It has some of that, true, but to my mind it also has elements of *Picnic at Hanging Rock*.

In recent years they have tried to emasculate the track layout but it's fair to say they haven't quite succeeded. It is fast, and dangerous, and it does have great consequences if you get it wrong, particularly once you have arrived at the end of Mountain Straight and begun the impossibly steep ascent to wind your way across the mountain to Forrest Elbow. Then again 'Con Rod' is fast and tricky in a cross wind, the wet or in traffic, but tracks need to be challenging and with some risk involved. That's what it's all about and that's why drivers feel they have accomplished something at the end of the race weekend. If it was all too easy, it would not have the same sense of fulfilment, that's how life is in many ways.

The chief engineer of years gone by, recently retired, spent many race seasons extending guard rails, improving run offs and trying hard to make it as safe as possible. He often asked me what I thought of his latest efforts and sought suggestions for future 'improvements'. Once he asked me what we

could do between 'Skyline' and 'the Dipper'. I said go to the council depot, get some drills and bore holes in that big hunk of rock that sticks out on the right hand side before you turn into the entrance of 'the Dipper'. He was thinking, 'Ah Brock wants to have it flattened, blasted to submission and removed.' How wrong he was, the next thing I said was, 'Go to the army disposals and get some knives and bayonets, glue them in the holes handle first, and let the blades glare menacingly at the competitors, that'll slow the buggers down.'

It took him some time to forgive me for this flippancy, however the point I was making is that the racetrack and the race itself is only respected by so many because of the awesome track layout. This is something that many motor sport administrators fail to comprehend, since their minds are usually hooked into dollar deals, TV rights and things of that nature.

There have been some peculiarities over the years, especially during the annual enduros, that smack of the organisers' unique approach. The first thing that comes to mind was the difficulty that all NON Australian Racing Drivers Club members had. Hell, I couldn't even get into the track the year after I'd won my first 'big one' at the Mount. The ARDC is a motor sport body of NSW and those from outside that state met some challenges.

Then there was the time they couldn't read '05', so I had to resort to '5' for the first few years. Apparently, '05' wasn't a real number in their rarefied atmosphere. Was it the elevation of the Mount? In '76 the race went to a tearful Bobby Morris; however subsequent lap counts agreed that it was won by John Harvey. They did finally acknowledge his win at his Testimonial Dinner late in 2002, but that wasn't 'official'.

Then there were the tray trucks bringing broken down and smashed cars back to the pits so they could later rejoin the fray. The only sign that they

were ahead was a stationary white flag indicating 'service vehicle on track'. I can tell you the sight of a truck tray lurking at windscreen height while floating into the Dipper or Forrest's Elbow did cause one to pay instant attention.

Speed differential? I get amused when I hear some current comments about some fellow Supercar driver being off the pace – say maybe eight or nine seconds or even 12 seconds per lap. How would they cop a nice easy minute per lap slower? It did happen.

I've always reckoned that passing and being able to negotiate slower traffic – judging when, where and how was (and is) a major part of race craft.

I would like to make one plea to racetrack officialdom. Deploy the safety car only when there are no other options left. Don't try to protect race drivers and their crews from themselves. If it's wet, it's slippery. If you reckon you can do it on slicks, well so be it! The choice and the subsequent outcome have to hang on the shoulders of the competitors, that's just the way it is.

That is what has made Bathurst great. It is a race that has assumed a place in our culture in this part of the world. A racetrack that is revered around the world. Wouldn't mind being out there myself zeroing in on Number 10."

Peter Brock
Herald Sun column
6TH OCTOBER 2003

Peter on the podium in 1972.

| 1972 Peter Brock's winning Torana XU1.

"I was a novice, hadn't yet learnt the ropes. It was the last time the race was ever run for standard production cars and the last time a solo drive was allowed. There's no doubt it was my weekend. I had a small, nimble Torana against Moffat's big heavy G.T.H.O Falcon, and it rained. I learnt a lot and it gave me faith and confidence in myself."

Peter Brock

"As mechanics, we considered ourselves extremely fortunate

because we had two of the three best drivers in the country. Moff was a Ford man and Colin Bond and Peter, Holden. Because Peter gave his all both in the race car and when he was in the workshop, he quickly earned the respect of the crew and therefore got the best out of us. Colin lived interstate and was allowed to do what he wanted when not racing, whereas Peter was being groomed by Harry Firth. This probably helped shape him into the excellent driver he became. However his charismatic approach to people was very different to Harry's and the crew responded accordingly.

The trip we took to Bathurst in '72 was memorable. Harry wanted us to run the cars in on the way up, besides we only had the use of one trailer which was Peter's. Once Harry had put XU1 wheels and tyres on it, it became his? Peter wanted to drive Colin's car at first to make sure both were the same spec. So we started out that way and then changed back so that Peter could become totally familiar with his car. We agreed to slip stream so that he could get the feel of the handling under those circumstances. This was at 100 MPH which was ok because there was no speed limit in NSW at that time. I kept an eye on his headlights in my rear view mirror but they suddenly disappeared. I thought he had stopped for a twinkle, and kept going for some miles before I thought it best to pull up and wait for him. To my complete surprise, there he was right on my bumper, driving by my tail lights, with no headlights and a wrecked windscreen!

The trip was slower from then on.

We eventually arrived in Bathurst and were in bed about an hour and a half before the boys arrived in the vans. It was a hasty trip to Bathurst Motors first thing in the morning for running repairs in time for the first practice session.

This was the start of a life long friendship of mutual respect and admiration."

Ian Tate

(Ran Peter Brock's workshop)

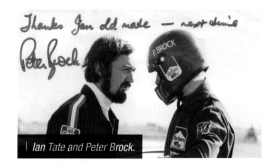

| Ian Tate and Peter Brock.

MOTOR RACING IS DANGEROUS. SPECTATORS
AND ALL PERSONS ATTEND THE MEETING
ENTIRELY AT THEIR OWN RISK.

"I was running as a privateer after a few years with the factory. It meant a total change in approach. We had minimal budget and backup. We stuck to our plan and ended up winning, which was pretty handy as it was needed to pay the bills."

Peter Brock

Peter and Brian Sampson **on the podium** with Evan Green and Bruce Hindaugh.
Bottom – Racing past the **spectators**.

Top – Peter cornering – slight lift of the inside wheel.
Bottom – Peter cruising to another Bathurst victory.

"I was back with the factory. It was relatively straight forward. We had a top crew, a top car and plenty of support. It was the easiest one so far."

Peter Brock

"Back in 1978 I got a call out of the blue

that resulted in my fully fledged appearance in the Australian motor racing scene. Greg Chambers who was then Peter's 'beancounter', as he was fondly called, had been given the task of calling to offer me the sum of $5,000 to drive with Brocky at Bathurst. It was too good a deal to walk away from, but I had no concept of just how big a deal it was to become. I actually ended up getting more than the five grand because we did really well and I got a percentage of the prize money as well.

It was an interesting time because while we won virtually everything, it still wasn't enough to cover the costs involved for the weekend, but that was motor sport in those days. At least I got paid, which was more than many did.

In many ways Peter and I were like peas in a pod. We shared a similar sense of humour and enjoyed many a laugh. The atmosphere in the team was fantastic which added to the enthusiasm. Peter did the majority of the laps and started and finished. This was fine with me after all, it was

his car and team. I jumped at the invitation to come back in '79 and once again it proved a dream come true. To have won that race by six laps and with Peter breaking the lap record on the final lap was something one can only dream of.

We never had a cross word between us and the rapport made racing a real pleasure. So when we backed up once more in 1980 I was absolutely thrilled when I had to stop for fuel close to the end of the race and Peter left me in to take the chequered flag. Nothing was ever said but it was a clear indication of his confidence and trust in me. I was rapt. 1981 wasn't to be but you can't win everything.

Peter's attitude to racing was so much like mine. He would drive anything, anywhere, any time just because he loved it. He wasn't afraid of looking like an idiot if it didn't work out, so he would race anything and drive rally cars on or off road. He would simply try his best no matter what. I recognised that zest in him instantly because it was exactly how I approached my racing. It was in our blood.

Peter Brock and Jim Richards on the Podium.
Opposite – The start of the 1979 race.

"This was more difficult than the previous couple. It was my first year as a team owner and proprietor of our Special Vehicles Operation and in hindsight, the win was quite significant.

It established both myself and the business interests in a way that hadn't been seen before. It wasn't a straightforward win by any means."

Peter Brock

We always shared a good laugh and some great stories. We both loved motor bikes, and Peter wanted to join a group of us one weekend when we were going out into the bush for a ride. We dropped by his place to collect him, us with all our gear and Peter comes out in jeans, a pullover and gum boots. Reckoned he didn't need anything else because that was what he used when he rode around the farm!

Off we went out into the bush and about a kilometre into the ride we went through a large, deepish puddle. PB's bike got stuck in the middle so he put his foot down to steady himself. His foot sunk in the mud, the water came over the top of his boots and he had to get off the bike and push it out of the puddle. I will never forget the look on his face as he looked me in the eye and suddenly remembered that he had a meeting he was supposed to be at!! With that, he turned around and rode off home.

He committed himself to upgrading his equipment after that, but was forced to stop the bike riding after one of his leading mechanics, Daryl Bromley, came off in the bush not long before Bathurst and suffered a severe broken arm. The guys came to realise that this was probably not a wise thing to be doing given the possible outcomes.

I write this as I am about to head off to participate in the very event that was Peter's undoing. He will probably be looking down and vicariously enjoying the ride along with me. There is no doubt that I will remember him with a tinge of sadness but with some incredible memories that can never be erased."

Jim Richards
(Co-driver 1978–1981)

Top – Completing another lap of practice, at Bathurst.
Bottom – Celebration with teammate Larry Perkins.

"For the next two years, it seemed like Bathurst and I had a very special arrangement. Both wins were a result of dedication, planning and never losing sight of the rewards to be gained from winning the most important race in Australia."

Peter Brock

"I actually remember nursing the car with a malfunctioning tail shaft for the last third of the '83 race. The TV people were onto it, but were sworn to secrecy as the opposition could very easily have caught me if they'd known I was in strife."

Peter Brock

Top – Grant Steers, John Harvey, Larry Perkins, Bob Hawke and Peter Brock on the podium after the 1983 win.

Left – The '05' car that started the race.

Right – The '25' car completed the race.

"A rare victory that was synonymous with the professionalism that HDT had. In the years before this, it was particularly fashionable to be seen in that way. The cars looked great, the pit stops were slick, the preparation and teamwork was the best around. Things worked out. We got a 1–2, but it looked a damn sight easier than it actually was."

Peter Brock

The famous 1–2 win for Mobil HDT.

On top of the mountain. (Coventry Studios – Graeme Neander)

"Sometimes things seem overwhelming. Hostile press, business bust-up, difficulties wherever one turned. I don't think anyone can really imagine just how things were when preparing for that race. Probably my biggest test in overcoming adversity and getting on with the job. I've always loved Bathurst, particularly in the wet, so I just finished up in 7th heaven. It worked out great."

Peter Brock

"He always expected me to give 100% effort

and in return gave me 100% of his time and ability. He could sometimes be hard to work with but this only made me try harder.

We were at Holden for the test of the new, first model Commodore at Lang Lang, Holden's testing ground. We were testing the car and PB said to me, 'You know, we could win the Repco Round Australia Rally in this thing.'

On that day we left with one thing in mind. 'Let's sweet-talk the Holden big wigs into giving it a go!' The seed was planted.

Peter Hannenburger, a young engineer from Opel in Germany, was very keen and so we talked to the MD. All was go! The result is history. We worked together a number of times, each of which was enjoyable even if we didn't always get the results we wanted.

Peter always gave his all and never once walked away from his very loyal fans. I always enjoyed being with Peter and Bev as they were both very kind to the people around them. When we were testing a car for the 1995 Round Australia, Peter convinced my son Steven to go and do a rally. Steven is now rated in the top 5 in Australia and currently has the number 5 on his car. So I can now thank Peter for all of the money I am now spending on the sport.

Peter and Bev will always hold a place dear to me and my family."

George Shepherd

(Australian rally champion)

"There's no doubt in my mind it was the greatest thing I've ever done in a car, and I'll never forget that event as long as I live."

Peter Brock

The challenge of the desert.

Opposite top left – Repco 05 driving past the crowds.

Opposite left – Peter celebrating the win with teammate Barry Ferguson.

Opposite top right – A very happy Peter Brock.

Top (left to right) – Rauno Aaltonen, Shekhar Mehta, Barry Lake, George Sheppard, Barry Ferguson, David Boddy, Wayne Bell, Noel Richards, Matthew Philip, Peter Brock.

Bottom – Arriving at a desert checkpoint in the Repco Australian Rally.

"I began collecting Brock HDT road cars

in the early '90s and had acquired five of them by the time I first met Peter Brock at a charity event in the mid-'90s. That night I had the chance to speak with Brocky and we discussed the possibility of building a replica of his first ever race car, the Austin A30. Our friendship really began while building the replica Austin along with Peter's son James. In the following years we would not only rally together in events such as the Finke Desert Race but also as teammates, as we did in the 1998 Round Australia Trial rally.

In the Targa Tasmania tarmac rally events, I accompanied him as team assistant – this actually proved challenging as Brock was difficult at the best of times to manage. I recall one evening driving PB, Cameron McConville and Steven Richards to a signing event at a Dealership in Launceston, Tasmania. Going down into Launceston on a wet road, out of the corner of my eye, I saw Peter's right hand slowly go to the hand brake, so I braced myself for what was about to happen. At 60kms per hour PB yanked on the handbrake. At that speed it required me to apply a lot of left hand down steering lock to keep the Holden Rodeo straight. What happened next was hilarious. Steven Richards leaned through to the front seat and applied a lot of left-hand pressure, with a closed fist into Brock's right arm. In a look of shock, Brock, eyes wide and bright, said, 'What the hell was that for?' Steven replied, 'What the hell did you pull on the hand brake for?' Brock then said, 'Just testing my mate PC's driving skills.'"

Peter Champion

Peter Champion and PB on the Finke River Rally.

Top – Driving the Australian Safari.

Left – Peter Brock and Ross Runnals in the Rodeo for the Australian Safari.

Right – Driving through the terrain on the Australian Safari.

"On rare occasions, Peter was able to find the time to combine his skill as a driver with his love of Australia's superb outback and, as a bonus, raise funds for the less fortunate in the community. So when the opportunity presented to drive in the Variety Club Bash that went from Bourke to Broome, he leapt at the chance. What gave this event even greater appeal was the fact that his mates, Farnham and Wheatley, along with their wives Jill and Gaynor in their own car, were also participating. They got down and dirty and had an absolute ball. Channel 7 came on board as a sponsor for Peter which ensured that there would be fantastic coverage of the entire event.

He had such an amazing time that he grabbed a second chance to participate, this time with his mate Alan Moffat. On this occasion he also got to enjoy the company of Normie Rowe and Jackie Love, which ensured that there were many occasions to 'sing and dance' on stopovers in far flung places. Peter was a natural at virtually

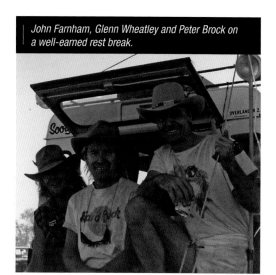

John Farnham, Glenn Wheatley and Peter Brock on a well-earned rest break.

anything he tried, but he was tone deaf and had little coordination when it came to dancing. This didn't stop him from joining in and entertaining the other competitors and locals when the opportunity arose."

Beverley Brock

John Farnham with the crew.

"The whole event is a challenge because the roads aren't formed like highways – it's a throwback to the old style with roads following local topographical features."

Peter Brock

Top – Targa Tasmania 2006.
Bottom left – Targa 1999 with son Jamie.
Bottom right – Peter with co-driver Anne Gigney.

Jamie and PB accepting the winner's trophy following the ute support race at the 24-hour race at Bathurst.

"I have been very fortunate in being born to the mother I have. Not only because she is

an amazing and beautiful mother but her relationship with one PG Brock led me to live a life that many an Aussie boy, or girl for that matter, would have given their eye teeth to experience, for even just a day or two.

I have had the pleasure and thrill of sitting next to Peter in many vehicles on the road, racetrack and country lane and those moments are something that I will hold dear until the day that I move on from this crazy planet.

I have memories as a kid of sitting in the back seat as we travelled home on a couple of particular steep and hilly roads, egging him on to go faster and faster until I literally vomited. It was like having your own personal roller coaster ride!

I also remember him bringing home his latest creation from down at HDT and doing some 'after hours' testing to fine tune the suspension around some familiar roads near home. To me, it felt like we were flying in some sort of space ship. Mind you, some people might say that PB confused that point at some times, too.

But even from that young age, I understood that there was something special about his ability to push a motor car to its limits. Obviously I was not exactly impartial about my dad as a kid, but as I grew up I had the opportunity as an adult to navigate and co-drive with him (much to his dismay). While he was, without doubt, the most awful back-seat driver – navigator ever, my opinion of his abilities was only reinforced.

I had the priviledge and honour of sitting next to him in competition through events such as the Targa Tasmania and the Australian Safari as well as in touring cars. Without doubt he was the best seat-of-the-pants driver I have ever seen.

I also believe that, for a long while anyway, he definitely had someone looking over him because he was able to do things in a car that I simply did not think possible. He may have said that 110% was all he knew and no other speed was possible. This would ultimately be his undoing but he would not have wanted it any other way.

What he will leave me with is the knowledge that if you truly believe in yourself and your abilities then anything is possible and to also bite off more than you can chew and then chew like hell!"

Jamie Brock

(Peter's son and co-driver)

"I was competing against him during the Round Australia Trial in 1995.

Pete was in a factory-backed Holden Commodore and I was running the Izuzu-GM Jackaroo Team. During one of Pete's many overtaking manoeuvres brought on because of his early troubles, he hit the rear of my teammate Peter Lockhardt's Jackaroo and destroyed the front of the Commodore. Pete had to be towed out of the stage while Peter Lockhardt drove on to the finish. I talked to Brocky after the finish and suggested that he'd best drive a Jackaroo next time.

When the 1998 PlayStation Rally Round Australia was announced, I approached Pete to drive our new Jackaroo. He had retired from V8 racing and to my surprise he said yes! Imagine the feeling of having someone you have respected and admired from when you were young, coming to join your

team. The guys in the team had no idea of the journey we were about to undertake with Brocky.

The first thing was to learn to manage the crowds lining up at every service point for Pete to sign autographs, glove boxes, steering wheels, and cars. We had to set up a table and chair away from the Jackaroos so the crew could service the car. Pete would be signing for hours or until he had to rejoin the rally. I was blown away by how much time he spent interacting with everyone while signing their chosen items. It was hard to tell who enjoyed the experience most.

I remember driving on the Nullarbor after just completing a 250km stage between Mundrabilla and Madura as I overtook a road train and struck up a conversation on the UHF radio. He was telling me that he loved motor sport and Brocky was his hero. After explaining to him that we were on a rally and that Brocky wasn't far behind (because he had got a puncture and neither he nor his navigator, Wayne Webster, had changed a tyre

in 20 years so it was going to take them a while to work out how to do it) the truck driver asked if Pete would sign his truck. If he pulled into the next service station I told him, I would ask Pete if he had time as this was only a short timed service point for the rally. Pete found a couple of minutes and I watched this six-foot, tattooed truckie turn into an admiring kid.

The effect Peter had on people amazed the whole team. One team member, Brent Twaddle, recounted this beaut story. At Hughenden there was a crowd waiting for Pete to arrive at the service point and he struck up a conversation with a lady in the line. She told him that they had driven 1,800kms to meet Peter. Her son was battling cancer and only had a few months to live. He was a huge Brocky fan and wanted to meet him before he died.

During the very short service stop Pete had taken up his usual position and was signing away. When Brent explained the story, Pete excused himself from the crowd and walked across the road and sat in the car talking to the young bloke until he had to continue in the rally. It was an extremely moving moment for the woman and her son. During this event Pete taught us a very humble and important part of living life.

He also had a calming effect on my driving and I went on to enjoy a lot of success. The highlight was competing in the Dakar rally. We had sat around the campfire at night talking and dreaming of competing in the Dakar together and how we were going to do it. When I did get to do it we achieved a great result in our first attempt. I felt Pete over my right shoulder on a few occasions telling me to calm down and drive sensibly.

I felt that what made Pete good was also what killed him. He'd start a race telling us he was just going for a drive and enjoy it without any pressure. But as soon as he could see a great result coming up, his competitive instinct would kick in and he'd try to win. He'd take lots of risks and crash the car.

Just like everyone else, I miss him and wish he was still here to tell stories and laugh out loud!"

Bruce Garland

(Rallying)

Above – Surveying the South Australia coast on the PlayStation Rally.

Opposite – With Bruce Garland on the Safari Rally.

"What a fantastic result, I have never seen a 24-hour race finish off like that. Two team cars, battling it out with a winning margin of only a couple of 10ths of a second... It's unbelievable – I am just over the moon. It is quite a long time since I stood up here in this position and I can tell you it is an excellent feeling."

Peter Brock

Top – Peter acceptance speech after winning the Bathurst 24-hour race.
Bottom – Close finish after 24 hours.

Left – PB and Dick Johnson eyeballing each other before the race.

Right – John Harvey, John Sheppard and PB.

"From the time that Peter first entered motor sport

in his unwieldy and unlikely winning A30 he attracted the attention of the crowd. It took several Bathurst wins and a change of temperament, however, before he cemented himself in the hearts of those same fans. His undivided attention to those loyal supporters coupled with his desire to help the wider community only added to his obvious driving talent.

For years he raced side by side in a gladiatorial manner with the likes of Allan Moffatt, Jim Richards, Dick Johnson, Glenn Seton and Larry Perkins without so much as swapping a layer of paint. They were all worthy rivals who shared mutual respect without the need to win at any cost. This attitude helped elevate Peter in the eyes of the young up-and-comers and he was dedicated to offering guidance whenever possible to any young blood arriving on the scene. His greatest and most successful understudy has been Craig Lowndes who took all of Peter's lessons to heart. Others, such as Neil Crompton, Brad Jones, Greg Murphy, the Kelly Brothers, Jason Bright and Garth Tander are just a few who were subjected to his 'lessons on life'. James Courtney was taken under Alan Gow's wing early in his career and received the benefit of the joint wisdom from the two mates and there were even times when Mark Skaiffe was on the receiving end of Peter's people skills.

His sincerity and commitment to encouragement and sharing of wisdom was not restricted to motor sport competitors. He also endeavoured to pass on the lessons he had learnt both on the track and in life to athletes, corporates and the general public whenever even a glimmer of an opportunity presented."

Beverley Brock

Top – A young Larry Perkins with PB.

Right – Arch rivals to teammates, PB and Allan Moffat came together from 1986 to drive for the Mobil HDT.

Left – PB and a young James Courtney at Gow's place in England.

Middle – PB and Mark Skaife in 1996.

Greg Murphy, Craig Lowndes, PB and Tomas Mezera celebrating on the podium in 1996.

"Peter was my motor racing hero

as a kid growing up, and of course my father worked on his cars back in the Holden Dealer Team days. But when I joined the Holden Racing Team, Peter really took me under his wing... I think because of the connection with my dad, because we came from very similar backgrounds and grew up in the same area, and because he had a genuine interest in helping young people.

Peter's influence on my career is immense. He taught me so much about driving the cars and showed me the 'tricks' to being fast on the tracks. Outside the car, though, he also taught me how to work within the team structure, and how to get the best out of myself and the team.

And, of course, I learned by watching the master, how to interact with the fans, the media and the sponsors... So much of who I am today and my success is because Peter showed me the way to do it."

Craig Lowndes

(Australian Touring Car champion)

CHAPTER FIVE

HOLDEN DEALER TEAM

"We started off with $10,000 and a few tools, basically. Looking back, I'm amazed we did things as well as we did straight off."

Top – "HDT" spelt by a collection of HDT cars at Lang Lang.

Opposite – Peter at HDT's Bertie Street home in Port Melbourne.

"You've just gotta do it and let the system catch up. If you can motivate people things happen. The proof of that is The Brock Organisation."

Peter Brock

"To tell you the truth, I thought we'd do the original 500 cars and then end up doing some specialised retail service work – we would be a performance-car centre, nothing more.

But it became apparent to me there was a real demand out there that manufacturers weren't satisfying.

For a whole lot of reasons Holden had gone past the days when it could build the L34 or the A9X. Holden couldn't build those sorts of cars anymore, but they could build a car we could turn into something special.

We started off with $10,000 and a few tools, basically. Looking back, I'm amazed we did things as well as we did straight off. When

I look at that first VC-based car, the overall package – handling, engine, styling – it was astonishing really. The hardest part was building a car within a system that had never built a car like that before – I mean, we were having to modify the engines after they had been manufactured, despite the fact we had type approval for them. To change that we then got some engines shipped on pallets, and changed over the cylinder heads and so on before shipping them back to the factory. We put a small cross on the timing cover of these so we'd know we didn't have to pull them apart when the cars arrived. It saved a tremendous amount of time and effort, but no one in GMH management really knew it was happening."

Peter Brock

Quotes from Street Machine's 'Brock' issue, 1988.

Top – The initial HDT VC Commodore. (Photo supplied by Brock Commodore Owners Club)

Middle right – VL Aero.

Bottom – Peter Brock's VC Commodore that Holden designer Leo Pruneau and PB worked very closely on. (Photo supplied by Brock Commodore Owners Club)

Peter Brock and the **HDT Special** Vehicles Team at the Port Melbourne **Office.**

"Peter was a good friend.

Although I had some input on his racing side, as Director of Design (Holden) my main association with Peter related to the various Holden cars he was modifwying.

Peter was a frequent visitor to Holden Styling, and I always took the opportunity to show him through the studios. He was like a kid in a candy shop. If Peter saw a new air dam or a hood scoop we were working on that took his fancy, it was always, 'Can you make me one?', which I frequently did. And if Peter had a body modification he wanted to try on the racing car, I would usually be able to produce a prototype model.

We were both very interested in aero-dynamics and had many ideas we wanted to try on the racing cars to improve their performance, but we could never get the design changes approved by CAMS' technical committee. It was always very disappointing.

Two Holden production cars that we worked closely on together were the VC HDT (Brock)/Commodore, and especially the VH 'SS' Commodore, with its various Peter Brock Group I/II/III modifications. These were real fun projects.

Holden Styling also had a lot of input on the look of the Holden racing team, designing many of Peter's racing suits, helmets and importantly the racing cars' livery, notably the red and white 'cigarette packet' Marlboro/HDT scheme.

Racing was Peter's life, but not many would know that he was also an artist. He could draw and paint, and had a good eye for design to make it all fit. Often he would talk about building a studio to pursue his artistic ambitions when he finished his racing career.

Peter Brock was a generous, charismatic individual, with a talent he could apply to whatever interests came his way.

One of my favourite Peter Brock stories: early on when Peter first started driving for Holden the Sales Department was interested in his popularity as a brand image for advertising purposes. Accordingly, Sales conducted a survey throughout metropolitan and rural Australia on brand recognition asking which out of Coca-Cola, Chevrolet and Peter Brock did those surveyed recognise most. When the results came in, Coca-Cola was the most recognised name but Peter Brock came in second, outdoing Chevrolet!

Not too bad for a guy from Diamond Creek..."

Leo Pruneau

(Holden Director of Design)

PETER BROCK

The World Test Car – VL Group A in the development stage.
(Photos supplied by David Whitehead)

"*Peter the Perfectionist!*

It was a fresh summer morning when I arrived at Dobler Chevrolet in America, and politely asked at the service reception to see our 'Howden Commodore Mate'. The guy was confused, but remembered there was a strange foreign car 'out back'. I made my way into the workshop, dragging a fuel line the length of a Commodore that had been flat-packed in a HDT spare-part box along with some more bits and pieces. I was carrying more parts for a Commodore than I was luggage.

Alas, there she stood, CWF-514, smeared in road grime and looking lonely. It was quirky to see the Victorian number plates amongst the sea of American domestic vehicles waiting patiently for their routine service. After getting the car on the hoist and separating the ensemble of Commodore parts from the underwear in my bag, the technician told me a bloke called Peter was on the phone.

Fair dinkum! It must have been some crazy hour back in Aus and I had only just arrived with a long list of improvements to the World Test Car at PB's direction. On the phone I was greeted by PB with his *latest* list of things to do. Even if he was distracted by the huge work/racing load back in Australia, he could still manage to unload a few more hours work for me (with no additional parts and a plan to depart NY on a five-day trip to LA early the next day!).

This was a prime example of the man who never rested or allowed an opportunity to pass in order to create the very best possible product bearing his name. Distance and time zone were no obstacle. It is an insight into how he felt about the VL Group A when all GM was after was his endorsement on a committee car. That company car was clearly well short of his own standards, hence enter the Director and the story of a lifetime!

We had many individual projects roll through the door at HDT, and PB had spent time on a Holden

Piazza, BMW 5 Series and, on this ocassion, a Nissan Skyline. We had spent the week fitting the bypass exhaust system and suspension components that philosophically made this car the same as a VL Commodore.

That weekend, for a change, I had plans with a new girlfriend which revolved around being home and chilling out. But Sunday sunrise was broken by a phone call from PB saying that he wanted to get into the workshop to make a change to the Skyline. At this point all the long hours, the lack of annual leave and the never-ending late hours had taken its toll. I limped into Bertie Street and opened the gates and donned the overalls.

PB announced that the rear shocker rubbers were a bit firm! 'Let's drill some holes in them to void the rubber and make them more compliant,' he said. Surely this could have waited until Monday! I was furious, speechless and emotional, to say the least!

Ten minutes of work on a Sunday morning had really pissed me off – this guy was crazy and obsessed and surely had better things to worry about. I bet he had gone to bed on Saturday night with the whole thing playing on his mind.

The exchange drew an uncharacteristically cold and grumpy response from me while he drove off with his normal enthusiastic smile. I stood there feeling drained and used.

But now I can see it wasn't about that shocker rubber; it was the attention to detail, the last millimetre, the last tenth of a second that made PB unique. He remained true to himself and left us a legacy of very special cars and motor racing memories. His famous quote that I take with me is, 'Davo, we are doing something that no one else on the planet is doing.'

David Whitehead
(PB's right-hand man)

"On a flight back from Honolulu to Melbourne, I realised that there were some interesting things that could well be applied to motor vehicles, because I had looked at some of the things that [our friend] Eric was doing with harmonising the human body by applying certain vibrations and getting some radical changes [in me, Bev and all his other patients].

All materials have their own energy vibration depending on what atoms they have. It was just being applied to the human body at this stage. I came back with the idea as to why it couldn't be applied to anything, an object. He was using crystals in a process called harmonics and this is... If you wanted to get a particular type of vibration you would use different crystals stacked on top of one another and then direct an energy force through the crystals, such as a light, and direct it through to the body below to alter the body's vibration at that spot. This was in about '85. We didn't know much in those days, but today science has gone ahead in leaps and bounds.

What struck me was that this could be applied to anything. Eric, Pauline, Bev and myself worked on this for a long time, intensely for 6 months nearly every night of the week up until 3 or 4 o'clock in the morning and then go and do our normal jobs. We were excited because we were seeing results. For me as an engineer/driver, I was stunned that you could get a change in a mechanical apparatus by simply using something that utilised free energy. So this full-on research was bearing a lot of fruit. It was stunning and as a race driver, I could feel that this road car was doing things that the laws of physics said were quite impossible. I thought it would be a matter of a few months and we'd have this thing sorted out and away we'd go. You have to look at it from

my eyes back in those days. How good would the road cars I was manufacturing be if I was to fit the device to every car we built. They would be exceptional, what a marketing advantage and it would be fair to say that throughout the entire research and development it was obvious that the type of device we should develop had to be in harmony with the environment, because let's be honest, things were starting to get questionable out there in the environment. Cars were never seen as being very compatible and as far as I was concerned, if you could make a motor car do all of the things that as a driver you wanted it to do and it was going to be environmentally friendly, then you were a long way towards developing a form of transport that truly did fit in with my view of what this planet was all about. We are building, digging up, manufacturing, and we are not really being too concerned how to balance the books.

So, there was a lot of good things about this particular product. We had no idea at the time what we were doing. We thought we were harmonising it. We are putting an energy in which is causing it to align in a certain manner and we are causing it to vibrate at a particular rate and we can alter that vibration by the frequency that was being transmitted which means if you were careful, you could eliminate certain vibrations which you didn't want. You could actually dial them out by putting in another vibration which cancelled out the other one. You could make a noisy car quiet and make the car ride smoothly and take out little squeaks and rattles. You could stop it at the source. So instead of actually eliminating the actual rattle you would work on the area that was creating the rattle in the first place. Much the same way as you work with the human body to eliminate cause and not effect. As time went by, it became obvious that this product was improving vehicles by a substantial percentage and we were starting to measure some very interesting results,

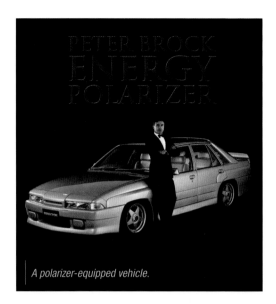

A polarizer-equipped vehicle.

measurable, not just subjectively. We ran a lot of blind tests with journalists running cars and they came back with the same impression that here was a car that did everything that you ever wanted it to do and it was an ordinary motor car rather than an exotic car built for that specific purpose.

Therein lay the problem. The moment that we turned around and said that this is what we are doing, this is how it works, we ran across a very mixed reaction. I suppose it would be fair enough to say that there were about 4 or 5 journos that were open-minded enough to accept it but the rest well and truly impossible, in fact like they said, explain it to us. If you can convince us then we will write the story. It is not up to me to convince anyone of anything as we all have our own belief systems. For a while there I did try to explain it but how do you explain something like that.

Those that don't want to know can cook up a bit of a storm for you. That is what happened of course with the whole energy polarizer debate. As time ticked by it was obvious that a lot of people were polarized by this particular activity. They either thought this is ok or no we don't like it.

So coming from a position of having a terrific product that produced all these great results to finding that people weren't ready for it, tuned into it and had this level of fear of it because of its unknown abilities. How was it powered? Why did it run? Who says it is ok to believe in it? If you ask any inventor of a new thing, they will say the same thing. The biggest problem you have to overcome is people's concern whether it is ok to support something. If you get enough scientific weight behind you for people to say, 'Yep! this is fine' this is terrific, people will eventually fall into the position of saying that this is a good idea. But it isn't all that easy, and in my naivity I believed it would be as simple as night follows day. It was inferred that I had gone off my head and all the time I am sitting back there thinking that I can't believe it because I have had this great idea. I am saner than I have ever been.

The only way people are going to be successful in life in the short term is to change their ways. It doesn't mean changing their business necessarily, it is just changing the way the business operates. Change your attitude to life. It's a fear-oriented society out there and I just don't let that affect me.

I let that whole polarizer fade away to oblivion back in '87 and yet to this day people remember that. It has stuck in their mind indelibly imprinted. They still can't quite figure it out as they know I wouldn't have been involved in it if there was nothing to it. It was a great idea. I just don't want to go into how it worked. If I had time all over again I wouldn't do it now because I can see that there is a means of achieving the same results without having the product sitting up there for all to see."

Peter Brock

CHAPTER SIX

THE SUPPORT TEAM

"You need a team that is pretty well tuned up, a car that is great and if you give it your best shot and achieve your full potential, winning could be a consequence of that successful activity. You all share in that experience, your crew and your sponsors and fans."

AUSTRALIA

December 6, 1993

TWR (Australia) Pty Ltd

278 Ferntree Gully Road

Notting Hill 3168

Victoria

Australia

Telephone (03) 544 0322

Facsimile (03) 562 9921

Mr P Brock
365 Doctors Gully Road
NUTFIELD   VIC   3099

Dear Peter

This follows our recent meeting and subsequent telephone conversation regarding our future relationship in our Company's Motor Sport program.

Subject to the completion of negotiations with our sponsors we would be pleased to enter into a Driver Contract with you on the following fee basis :

(a) A driving Fee of $125,000 p.a.
                        and
(b) A Sponsorship Attraction Fee of $72,000 p.a. *PROVIDED THIS DOES NOT CONFLICT WITH EXISTING CONTRACT ARRANGEMENTS* ✓ß

The Sponsorship Attraction Fee would provide the Team with the opportunity to market your services and time for the purpose of generating income for the Team.

We would require your confirmation that under the Sponsorship Attraction program any funding generated would not be subject to any claims by another party, e.g. Advantage International.

We have been specifically requested by Mobil to obtain your agreement to the above by Wednesday December 8, 1993. To comply with their request I would appreciate you faxing me by Wednesday December 8, 1993 on fax number 544 6446 your agreement to the above so that final agreements/contracts can commence to be prepared and executed when all sponsorship details are in place.

Should you have any queries on this matter, please give me a call beforehand. For the purposes of timing, this copy has been faxed and the original will be with you tomorrow.

We look forward to hearing from you.

Yours sincerely

JOHN A CRENNAN

AGREED : _____ (P BROCK)

8/12/93

"During the early months of 1949,

a small, knock-kneed boy and two of his young friends stood on a dusty corner in the middle of a one horse town. They were waiting with great anticipation, not taking their eyes off a place in the distance, down a narrow road that meandered past the railway station, down a slope and past the local garage where they were observing. The car finally appeared.

It was a new vehicle for the local postmaster at Strathewen and the kid's patience was rewarded. It was a highlight, not only of the day but the year and the decades beyond. I still clearly remember the '48 series Holden that motored beautifully by the late afternoon in Hurstbridge. It was the first in the district and well I should remember it since it was sold by my father Geoff from a small garage, which still stands on the corner in main street.

Shortly after, we received our own 48 series, registration number PV 159. A svelte black machine that topped 83 MPH down an incline at nearby Kangaroo Ground, no doubt aided by much encouragement from yours truly and other members of our family as we urged Dad on. I could not begin to give a complete story here of my involvement with 'Australia's own'. Suffice to say that it was quite simply part of my life and that of my family.

When it came time to have a go at motor sport, my inspiration was the myriad of Holden's racing in the 60's, 48's, FJ's FE and finally the fabulous EH S4. The call of motor racing was insistent, the gizzards of a wrecked HD 179 M into a poor unsuspecting Austin A30. It was ugly, unwieldy and cheap, but it went like the wind. It weighed 1600lb and had 240 BHP!

Then came the fateful day when one Harry Firth called to invite me to race for his new team. The Holden Dealer Team. I had been racing for a mere 18 months, but it seemed an eternity of waiting. My prayers had been answered, I could still park the car in the driveway at Mum and Dad's, I was going to race a Holden. From Monaro's to XU1's, L34's, A9X's and every permutation of Commodores, I've raced just about the lot. Even Panel Vans and Kingswoods.

How many have I owned, driven and raced? I honestly don't know, but I do know it has been a wonderful experience, one I am grateful for!"

Peter Brock

Above – Driving back the years, with (top) the EH 1965 and (above) 1969 HT 350 Monaro.

Previous page – Peter Brock at the new Team Brock emergence.

"Peter and I shared one love more important than Holden – Collingwood.

Bathurst was usually scheduled on the weekend after the AFL (VFL) Grand Final, but in 1977 Collingwood drew with North Melbourne, so there was a replay on the Saturday of Bathurst weekend. Peter finished practice on Saturday morning, then let it be known that the GF replay would on in his motel room. There was a pile of fish 'n' chips, beers, one crappy TV, two Collingwood supporters (Peter and me), and about 25 other blokes, none of whom barracked for North Melbourne, but they all hated Collingwood. It was a bad afternoon, but Peter and I had bonded.

Having become the Marketing Manager at Holden in the '80s, life with Brock became a little more formal, but with Peter things were never too formal! I soon realised that Peter Brock and Holden were closely paralleled in their true identity and qualities. Australian to the core – larrikin, no fancy airs and graces, a 'get it done, no matter what' attitude, tough, reliable and, above all, fair dinkum.

Peter was mercurial. Those moments of genius that we all saw in his racing also came out in business. He had the genius to see the opportunity for performance-enhanced Holdens and the nouse to build a low-cost, go-fast car. What Peter didn't have was the ability to manage a company bureaucracy like Holden, so he relied on a few key executives in Engineering and Marketing to help steer his proposals through.

Holden's sales success was absolutely linked to racing success and very much personality-driven by Peter. Holden Commodore was personified by Peter and became Australia's top-selling car for over 20 years.

Peter also had a magical flair for PR. In an era where spin-merchants came into their own, Peter had the ability to cut through. My most memorable recollection was, when faced with extreme vitriol about building performance-enhanced cars that were excessively fast, Peter responded on TV and radio, 'You really don't understand our target market. They are only interested in driving down Toorak Road at 10 km/h and looking at themselves in the shop windows.' This was the absolute truth.

Peter was an amazing person. Many people loved him deeply, as I did, because he personified the real Australian, not someone of great education or business or political achievement. He was more the Aussie battler made good, but somehow better than that. In that respect, he reminds me of Don Bradman, and I think Peter is deserving of equal admiration."

Ross McKenzie
(Executive Director Sales, Marketing and Aftersales,Holden Limited: 1998–2006)

Peter Brock in his Holden Racing gear.

"I vividly recall my very first meeting

with Peter Geoffrey Brock. I had just been promoted to Advertising & Sponsorships Manager with responsibility for HDT. I drove the short distance from Mobil's offices in South Melbourne down to Bertie Street, Port Melbourne.

Upon arrival at the Team's office's, one of Peter's latest creations – his iteration of a Holden-based road car was sitting, gleaming on the showroom floor. I admired the fine lines and attention to detail while I waited. People were coming and going and there was a really positive vibe and creative atmosphere. Peter was running a little late so I was taken to the boardroom area where I was introduced to Beverley Brock. It was clear and apparent from the start that Bev played a significant role in Peter's life and in the success and health of the business. I have enormous respect for Bev both professionally and personally. The multitude of challenges that came her way and how she handled them with style, grace and dignity are things that I will always remember.

Peter eventually arrived, having been in a meeting with the race team. You hear of people having star quality but until this moment in my life, I had not met anyone as charismatic and inspiring. Our first meeting was spent with me introducing myself and then listening to Peter talk about his business, racing, current issues and challenges. Peter gave me a tour of his facilities, culminating in a visit to the race team. It was here that I met the legendary and incomparable Graeme 'Mort' Brown, the team's manager, and other key team members.

After this meeting I was struck by the enormity – the scope and value of Mobil's sponsorship. The potential of leveraging Brock's iconic brand to help build Mobil brands was clear in my mind. This was a sponsorship coup! Given that Mobil remained principle sponsor of the team for many, many years and continues to be a sponsor today some 30 years later is testimony to the legacy of this sponsorship.

Since 1985 and until his untimely death, Peter Brock was involved with Mobil in virtually every part of the business. He was the face of Mobil retail products but he had enormous pulling power in all areas including aviation, wholesale, commercial and industrial products. He was a regular 'star' at Mobil functions across Australia and internationally – if Mobil was involved, then Peter played a role. Whenever Peter was a guest speaker, there was never an empty seat. Along with the enormous PR value Peter also provided technical help.

His ability to relate and communicate with people, all ages, all sexes, no matter what their status was remarkable. Quick, witty, intelligent, charismatic and credible are just some of the few superlatives that can describe him. His natural creativity and curiosity about how things work and about life made him inspirational and a pleasure to work with. All combined, Peter was indeed 'Perfect' not only on the racetrack but also as the face of the sponsor.

The Polarizer issue and the acrimonious split from GMH did serious harm to Peter on so many levels. The ugly side of journalism...cutting down the tall poppy.....corporate greed...lost friendships and indeed so many horrible things happened at that time. Peter and his business virtually collapsed. Had it not been for Bev, a few very loyal and supportive people and the decision of Mobil to continue its sponsorship, the business may well have folded. I am so very happy at a personal level that Mobil's management elected to do so. 'Sticking' with Brock during this time could have adversely affected us also, but the Australian public rewarded us through this period.

This was a curious result given that after a lifetime of racing GMH products and being inextricably tied to Holden, Peter switched to BMW M3s and then to Ford Sierras. So loved by the public he was even accepted in a rival product – such was the brand strength of PG Brock.

Did Mobil get value from this sponsorship? Absolutely no question. I believe that the return on this investment was far in excess of what we ever dreamed of. Personally, I valued my time working with Peter and the team. I got so much out of this experience with the greatest being that of the day of Peter's final victory at Bathurst October 3rd, 1987, my son Matthew was born. He is my reminder of those very special days."

Nick Hluszko

(Mobil Advertising and Sponsorship Manager)

PB with the 1985 Group A Commodore V8.

PB with a 1985 winner's laurel.

"Legend, champion, pain in the ass.

You know, Peter was a great bloke. He was a superstar behind the wheel, a natural; he would never shy away from a chat with anybody. As any of you Brockologists would know, he was famous for the amount of time he would spend signing autographs and chatting to anyone who came along. He had a presence. Everyone shut up and took notice when he walked in to a room. He was to a racing team what Gary Ablett or Chris Judd is to an AFL team. He was an inspiration and a god in the motor racing fraternity.

Righto, enough of the bullshit. Brock was a fantastic, natural gifted driver and great at kissing babies (also a few named after him by the way, not his though, I don't think). But, he also could be very hard work. Like anyone at the top of their profession, Peter had demands. If he did not get what he wanted he could very much be the spoilt kid. Ok, he owned the operation, and you would think that the owner gets what he wants. To a point, yes. But there were many times when his want or enthusiasm had to be contained or controlled for the good of the race team's future. Peter went through quite a few very frustrating, financially unrewarding years after his split with GMH in 1986. Inside the race team we still tried to supply him with the best equipment that our budgets would allow. Through the '80s and '90s we had a great group of people working for us, both in the race team and the HRT/Brock cars business. All of these people were driven by belief in 'the icon', 'the master'; some called him 'the Bahgwan' for some reason!

Brock was fortunate enough (through his own hard work) to attract Mobil Oil Australia as a major sponsor in 1985. Mobil had great faith in Peter and time has shown that this company was a great supporter of his and motor racing in general. Mobil got Peter through the hard times and continued to support him up until his untimely end. From my point of view, this company treated Peter and the race team as family and guarded us all through some very turbulent times.

Mobil Oil the company used to appoint 'sponsorship managers' to liaise with the race team and Peter on a day-to-day basis. Over the period of 10 years we had several sponsorship managers who were all fantastic people to deal with. The one great guy who I would dearly love to dedicate this section to is Mobil sponsorship manager – Mr Ken O'Brien. Ken passed away in May 2011 and we are all very saddened by this loss. You know how I mentioned about Peter being an inspiration earlier. That is exactly the effect he had on our mate Ken. 'Kob', as he was affectionately known, worked at the coal face alongside Peter's long-serving 'lady of everything', Colleen Adamson, to ensure that Brock was Brock and everything ran smoothly and Peter got what he wanted (quite often a pain in the ass) and Mobil got what they wanted. Thanks Kenny, and I hope you both are somewhere nice having a beer and talking crap as we all did."

Graeme 'Mort' Brown

Team Manager

PB with 'TEAM ARMOR ALL' promotion team.

Below – PB filming the Armor All Rain Dance ad when the drought struck and washing of cars was restricted.

"Peter was more than the official
spokesperson for Armor All, we became friends.
He was always genuinely interested in what we
were doing from a business perspective and what
we were up to in our lives
outside of work.

He helped me to gain a better appreciation for
cars, motor sport and life and this was often
over a cup of peppermint tea. Peter had the
ability to make you feel special. He gave you that
reassurance that you could achieve whatever you
put your mind to and to 'follow your dreams'."

Paul Blair
(General Manager – Australia, New Zealand)

"Bridgestone's association

with Peter Brock spans back to the early '70s. It was an easy decision to continue sponsoring Peter for so many years because he was so recognisable and loved by the public. He was popular both among motor sport fans and non-enthusiasts alike. He had very broad appeal, to both young and old, and equally to men and women.

I believe that the reason for his popularity was due to his humility. He was the peoples' racing-car driver. He always had time for people – which posed a challenge if you were in a hurry. But Peter did not care too much about time.He would spend hours signing autographs for fans and made sure no one was left out. Above all, Peter had a soft spot for the underprivileged. He would make sure that he spent more time chatting to these people and always wrote a word of encouragement for them in his autographs.

Peter would ring me a few times a month. His mind was always ticking and he always had some great idea. Some of his ideas were good, but I did not have the heart to tell him about the others. He was always so enthusiastic and keen to try new things. He was not afraid of failure."

Stanley Toh

(General Manager of Marketing – Bridgestone Australia)

Peter's Bridgestone sponsor in the Gown Hindaugh days of '73.

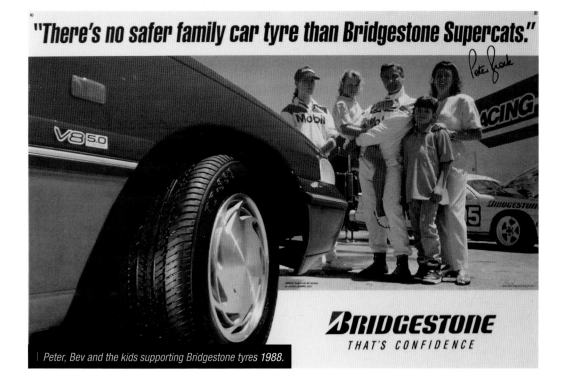

"There's no safer family car tyre than Bridgestone Supercats."

BRIDGESTONE
THAT'S CONFIDENCE

Peter, Bev and the kids supporting Bridgestone tyres *1988*.

Top – The 'Marlboro Team' photo shoot.

Left – Peter with Levi's promotional girls.

Right – Peter sitting on top of the Marlboro truck.

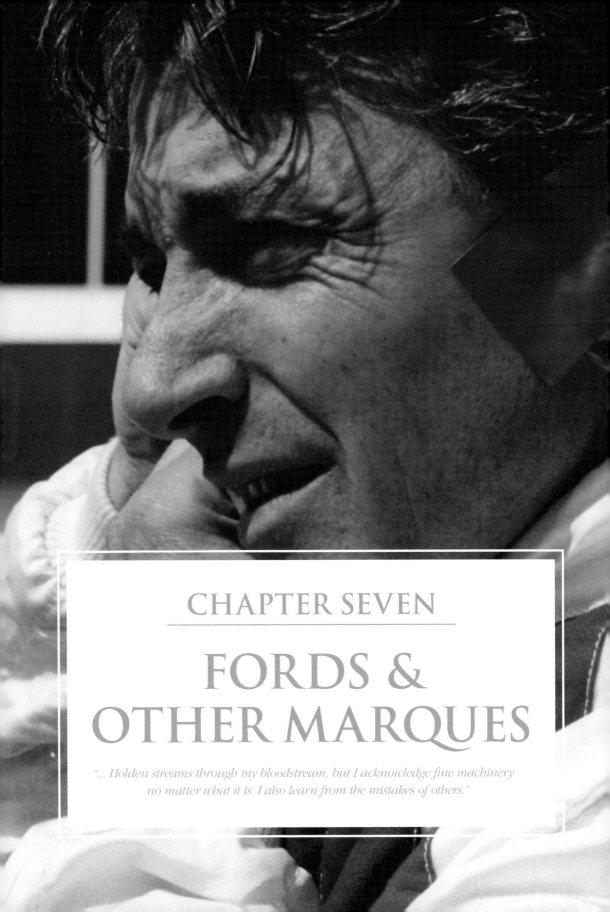

CHAPTER SEVEN

FORDS &
OTHER MARQUES

"... Holden streams through my bloodstream, but I acknowledge fine machinery no matter what it is. I also learn from the mistakes of others."

LE BROCK. LE PORSCHE. LE MANS.

BOB JANE TEAM AUSTRALIA
Peter Brock & Larry Perkins.
Porsche 956.
Le Mans, June 16-17, 1984.

| Brock and Perkins 1984, Le Mans.

"In 1975 Peter was given the opportunity

to drive a BMW at Kyalami in South Africa. What red-blooded racing enthusiast would turn his back on such an invitation? He had no money, was reliant on sponsorship to make it possible but was determined to make the most of every opportunity. Then in 1976, he entered the BMW in the 24-hour race at Le Mans but was forced to retire while leading his class. The brief experience was a gift and broadened his horizons considerably. It gave Peter a taste of the BMW motor car which later became his choice of race car.

In 1977, Peter was given the opportunity to co-drive with Gerry Marshall at the Spa 24-hour race in Belgium. It was seen as one of the lesser cars in the field but with the two at the wheel driving through a huge range of conditions, they came second in one of Peter most exhilarating

experiences behind the wheel. In some ways Peter likened the Spa track to Bathurst which is why he enjoyed driving there whenever he could.

Grant Steers, better known as 'the Spear', Peter's long time housemate and Holden employee, was with him in Spa. He needed to get into the track on one occasion without his passes so wore an army shirt he'd bought from an Army Disposal store in Australia and strode through officials pointing officiously at the rank on the shirt. The poor officials let him through!

Gerry, 'the Whale', was to later race for Peter at Bathurst in 1977 the year he ran a three-car team. Peter also had brief flings with specialist race cars when the opportunity presented itself.

In 1981 there was a second attempt at Le Mans per favour of Alan Hamilton. The car looked superb and the driver lineup was awesome with Jim Richards

PB at the Lada Convention in, of all places, country Victoria.

Jim Richards, Colin Bond with *Peter* inside the car at Le Mans, 1981.

Opposite top – Peter at Bathurst, 1988.

Opposite right – Peter and BMW in Germany, 1988.

and Colin Bond joining the challenge, but problems with the gear box meant the car failed to qualify.

Bob Jane had Peter drive his Monza in 1982 in a series against Alan Jones just after Alan had won his World Championship. Bob also backed a third attempt at the Le Mans 24-Hour in his Porsche 956 in 1984. Bob and his supporters joined Peter and his team to stay in a beautiful 600-year-old Chateau some 45 minutes drive from the circuit. It was an incredible event that eventually came to an end in the early hours of the morning when Larry Perkins ended up in the catch fence while trying to overtake a slower car just past the start/finish line.

These forays into other makes were just a flirtation brought on by opportunity. They were to be enjoyed, valued and learnt from but the vast majority of his racing was in the GM product which was embedded in his psyche.

In 1987 the wheels fell off that relationship and there was no way that Peter could run a Holden. He was crushed but defiant. Dealers were forbidden to support him and there was no way he could access spare parts. He had gone from being the Golden Haired Lad to the absolute outcast.

An enormous void was left in Special Vehicle manufacturing and motor sport. At that time, the John Player Special team run by Frank Gardener was up for sale. Frank's health was in decline and BMW were offering great support. Ron Meacham, the head of the organisation, was keen to see Peter take over the team and venture into creating special kits for road cars. A price was determined and a relationship forged. Meetings were held with the German heads of the organisation while in Spa in 1987. Everyone was rapt in the future. However 1988 proved it to be a short lived affair.

The regulations were changing and the BMW was no longer a competitive vehicle that fitted the new rules. Shock of shocks, discussions were held with the Ford executives in Australia.

At the same time, with no Holdens available to continue the creation of Special Vehicles and over 80 staff to be concerned about, it was a time to explore other options. Many offers were being made to the struggling business and it was recognised that the Holden side of HDT could well continue in someone else's hands. It was Peter that the parent company was at odds with. Holden had established their own set-up in creating Holden Special Vehicles which is what they had wanted for some time. It was known to be a lucrative business and they wanted to have control over whatever was produced. So the working and historical part of HDT was sold off in a deal that was to be less than tasteful. The purchasers paid a deposit only and then through a legality, found that since the company name had been changed in the process they didn't have to pay the balance. Needless to say, Peter chose not to have anything to do with the new owners of HDT. It changed ownership on several occasions and is now in the hands of Peter Champion, a long time and trusted friend who has coupled the business with the museum he created in Peter's memory.

Australia was endeavouring to balance trade with Russia at the time, and the opportunity presented itself to get involved with Russian cars. The Lada Niva was no example of fine, classic machinery, and it leant itself to easy refinements to both its performance and visual appearance.

It was a most curious time as it seemed that in both football and motor racing, allegiance to a team or brand no longer held sway. Everything was fluid. In simple terms if you wanted to be in the winners circle, which meant ensuring sponsorship, you needed to be in a competitive vehicle. So, Sierras were it. Mobil and the other sponsors were happy and the team made the necessary adjustments. It just went to show that when a move is necessary, anything is possible. Even a Ford!

The Russian connection was sold off and the newly established business, Austech Automotive, set up in Coburg, Melbourne. As money was incredibly short, a partnership was established with Alan Gow who had so generously donated his time and expertise to Peter during the separation from Holden. A small number of Ford vehicles were made including Mavericks and Fairlanes. However, it was determined that Peter was better off out of business all together. While he was a designer and amazing developer of road cars, he was not cut out for the cut and thrust of the business world.

Throughout this time his motor racing was also undergoing change. While Peter was no longer building Holden cars there were small steps being made to re-establish the links with his beloved Holden. Their research was constantly showing that the public would always see the two linked and Peter was once again doing company visits and speaking at vehicle launches. The nature of these outings was very much controlled by the company, so Peter approached them to make sure they didn't object to his driving a Volvo. He was given the go-ahead to do just that and his first drive occurred at the Australian Grand Prix.

There was a huge outcry, probably whipped up by a disappointed public who had never abandoned Peter and still saw him as a Holden man. This made what was a most agreeable personal relationship between Peter and Volvo once again short lived.

The Holden Racing Team had been struggling. At Bathurst in 1993, when their team faced major problems getting their car to the start line, Peter offered his and his crew's assistance, in an act of grace. It was noticed by John Crennan, head of the enterprise then, who offered a hand of 'forgiveness' and invited Peter back into the team for the following year. It's fair to say the alliance with John was always a wary one. John certainly recognised the value of Peter's public appeal and the effect that had on sales of merchandise which went a long way towards funding much of the team's activities. He also needed the income that Peter's long-time sponsors would bring because where Peter went, his sponsors followed.

Peter was once again back in the fold, but in a very controlled way. He devoted himself to racing without the distraction of business as that was not allowed under the terms of his contracts. He raced with Tomas Mezera, Craig Lowndes, Greg Murphy and Mark Skaife throughout those final years along with Jason Plato and Derek Warwick in the Vectra. When that all finished there came opportunities to participate in the newly established Nations Cup racing Monaros which gave him his much heralded 10th Endurance race win at the mighty Mountain.

So he started and finished his professional career in the brand that was a part of his cellular make up. However, interspersed in that period of time were wonderful encounters with many fine and some not so fine marques of cars. It is probably best not to even discuss the final vehicle he drove, which by his own description, was a brute of a car to handle. It was a challenge to drive and one he wanted to take on in order to tame it and give it the Brock touch!!!

Sadly for all who knew him, the opportunity to refine the car never came."

Beverley Brock

Above – Brock at the Lada Convention with the Russian Trade Delegates.

Opposite – PB with Mobil grid girls in the Sierra.

"Annoying enthusiasm...

I guess that pretty much sums up Peter. I have never before, or since, met someone who has anywhere near the level of enthusiasm that Peter had, particularly when he first gets into something. It could be a race car, a road car, a new boat, a new house, new race-team shirts or even building a new dam at home – if he believed in it, then he would throw himself into it with such boyish enthusiasm that it was useless to try and temper him.

A prime example was the Lada car from Russia. Back in the '80s these cars were, to put it mildly, a piece of crap. Peter had a go at trying to make them better – even producing a few 'Brock Lada' versions. Attempting to fettle that car into being a great car would be like Lucianno Pavarotti trying to make a great opera singer out of Sam Newman. A nice idea but always doomed to failure.

The first time a 'Lada Samara' appeared at our Bertie Street premises for evaluation, I took it for a lap around the block and, within yards, realised what a pile of junk it was. Peter turned up and we smugly sent him off for a drive in the car, knowing he would come back dismayed and shocked at its poor dynamics, poor build quality and...errr, poor everything.

After about 30 minutes he arrived back and said, 'Not bad....we can do something with this!' And with that, Peter took the Lada off into his special area of the premises, where he spent days/weeks modifying, improving, adjusting, testing and bringing the car up to a better standard. After which, it proudly displayed the famous Brock Signature and became one of the rarest Peter Brock 'special vehicles' ever built.

Don't get me wrong – it was still a piece of crap. Only now it was a slightly better piece of crap. And there would have been only one person in Australia that could see merit in that car – because only one person had that annoying enthusiasm that so often overcame reality; Peter Geoffrey Brock.

And that's the way he attacked his life; with such annoying enthusiasm that it would leave most of us behind in his wake. When Peter wanted to do something it was futile to try and stop him. But even after all these years since his passing, I still wish I could make those futile attempts...it was annoying, but fun. There is only ever going to be one Peter Brock in our lives – and thank gawd I was part of it."

Alan Gow
(Business Manager – British Touring Car Championship)

Left – Alan Gow and PB at Gow's house in England.
Opposite page – PB in 1989.

| Grant Steers admiring...PB's Torana!

"In 1977 Peter and I went off to London,

which was my first real overseas travel (and I truly felt that New Zealand was the best place with the best people in the whole world, bar none).

I was working for the general in Australia and organised the loan of a car from Vauxhall, our GM company in England. Peter was set to team with Gerry Marshall in the Spa 24-hour Francorchamps in Belgium.

The Spa track is virtually the same as they race it today except that it was the original 14-mile length. Gerry drove us around the track on our arrival, which was amazing. He had placed there the previous year. On Peter's first flying lap in practice he beat Gerry's best time by over one second.

It was a race with constantly changing weather conditions where it could be pouring rain through the forest section and totally dry on the main straight. At one stage Peter had a very scary moment when he aquaplaned while holding the little car in a tight line right through the downhill sweeper coming out of the forest.

The team had lousy wet weather tyres and no chance of getting any others so I went and bought a good set of wets to help them along. They ran 4th overall and won their class in that two-litre midget of a car.

It was a new experience for me as they had a bar in the middle of the track that crew and drivers alike could get a drink throughout the race! I had never seen that sort of thing before and while Peter and I both smoked and drank at the time, we never indulged but I am sure that Gerry took full advantage of the facility. There was no breath testing of drivers at the race!!!

On returning to London we had a few days to fill in before our scheduled return flight. We needed to find accomodation and made the quickest tourist circuit of all time with Peter pointing out Big Ben, the Tower Bridge and Buckingham Palace, after which he stated that London doesn't have anything else to see. He kept driving and I would run in to potential accomodation to see if they had any rooms. This went on for about an hour until I found one room in an old-fashioned hotel right in the middle of London. Peter discovered that Australia was playing in a test at Trent Bridge the next day. 'Where's Trent Bridge?' I asked. 'It can't be far 'cos it's not a big island!' So off we went...

I will never forget the queues to get in. They went all around the ground twice from both directions. Undaunted, we went straight to the window by saying, 'Sorry, but we are from Australia and have to get in!' It was such a tiny ground that 30,000 spectators would overfill it. I personally don't recall much about the cricket but we stayed all day. Peter loved his cricket almost as much as his beloved Collingwood Footy Club.

The trip was a great experience. We also went to visit GM with the Polarizer and boy, is that another story!!!"

Grant Steers
(GM Sales Promotion Manager 1971–2004)

CHAPTER EIGHT

RETIREMENT & THE JOURNEY FORWARD

"Is it time to step aside and leave it for the young blokes? Maybe it is time for me to do other things. I am always up for change because if you don't then things go downhill. Who knows what the future holds, all I know for sure is that I will create my own reality and enjoy every moment!"

Peter Brock

Peter relaxed and all smiles before his 'first' retirement race.

"Having reached the momentous decision

to retire during the Touring Car Championship race at Winton in 1997, there followed a year of enormous activity and excitement tinged with uncertainty. The timing of the announcement would mean that he would still get to race in every state throughout the remainder of the year, thus giving him the opportunity to say his farewells to his devoted fans around the country.

There were record attendances at every meeting with many determined to see Brocky race for the final time. The year was filled with testimonial dinners, and amazing events at each and every race track. Peter made the promise at the announcement of his impending retirement that he would not leave the tracks until every person who wanted his autograph had received it. There was such an incredible outpouring of emotion. Grown men in tears. His final Bathurst was an unbelievable event with a record and highly emotive crowd."

Beverley Brock

Above – Peter and Bev, Alexandra and Sam McIntosh on the lap of Honour at Peter's final race at Oran Park.

Below – Peter and Bev listen to John Davidson's farewell speech, which brought tears to Peter's eyes.

"Driving is an art form, be grateful for the freedom it allows. Be tolerant and accepting, enjoy it."
Peter Brock

THE PETER BROCK FOUNDATION

Jamie, **Bev**, **Alex**andra, PB and Robert at the launch of **the** Peter Brock Foundation.

Peter decided very early in his retirement that there needed to be a way of harnessing the enormous goodwill generated throughout his career in a manner that would benefit the community. So the concept of the Peter Brock Foundation took form.

Beverley Brock

"Just after Peter announced his retirement from professional racing,

I picked he and Bev up from Sydney airport to shoot a television commercial. I started talking to Peter about how Bridgestone Australia would like to give back to society for their great support of our products. Peter then suggested that we should partner with him in supporting the Peter Brock Foundation which he had just established. That was the conception of one of Peter's better ideas.

Peter and Bev had always opened their home to underprivileged kids and people in need. So it was only a matter of time before this was formalised by way of the Peter Brock Foundation. The mantra of the foundation was to support the underprivileged in society and to help the cause of other charitable organisations.

After the television-commercial shoot, I followed up with Peter on how we might bring this idea to fruition. One of the charities that the Peter Brock Foundation supported was the Leukaemia Foundation.

A meeting was set up with the Leukaemia Foundation in Adelaide and we quickly found a link between a great need and the business of Bridgestone Australia. The Leukaemia Foundation had a need to transport patients to and from hospital for treatment in clean and comfortable vehicles so as to minimise their vulnerability to the environment. The idea was birthed that Bridgestone Australia would provide vehicles to transport leukaemia patients and the cars would be dressed up in racing livery to indicate support from the Peter Brock Foundation.

Today, 10 vehicles are in operation throughout Australia, providing much needed transportation for leukaemia patients to receive treatment. Peter and Bev spent a big part of their lives caring for the needy. The legacy of Peter Brock continues to this day, conceived from an idea that reflects the heart of Peter Brock – to care for the needy and underprivileged."

Stanley Toh

(General Manager of Marketing – Bridgestone Australia)

Clockwise from top – PB with junior motor cyclists; with the Mt Evelyn Fire Brigade; at Brock's Big Day Out with Glen Seton; and with primary school students at Katherine in NT.

"Brocky's Big Day Out became an annual event that combined a car show, market and auction. It was initially run at the Yarra Glen racecourse and became established as a fantastic opportunity for owners of car clubs of every marque to display their beautiful machinery and join in the fun of a bumper fundraising day. Local charities and community service groups were invited to attend so the benefit could be shared between the wider community.

Wherever possible, if Peter was asked to speak at a function, it was organised so that funds raised on the night were split between the local community and the PBF. It was a recipe for success.

Time and situation have changed. It became necessary to employ paid staff. The board has changed several times. Initially, with Peter's passing, it was a boom time for the foundation to flourish. It later became essential to direct the proceeds raised to a particular interest of Peter's, which was Driver Education and Road Safety issues. It became too labour intensive to administer the numerous claims from the many individuals in need.

There are opportunities to remember Peter in meaningful ways that are being explored. Peter was always looking for new ways to achieve his objectives as he frequently acknowledged that change is the only constant in life. The future is rich with possibilities which unfold with each new day."

Beverley Brock

| Brock's Big Day Out at Yarra Glen racecourse.

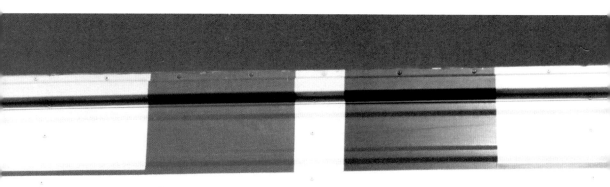

"I had left HDT after six years"

"I had left HDT after six years with them, the HDT team management felt it was time for me to go overseas for a while and get to know and see other things. I had gone to England and forged relationships with the guys from Vauxhall and had done a few races over there.

The initial version of Team Brock first came about in 1975 after I had won Bathurst as an independent and had beaten the official works team. Holden had produced another movie about my win at Bathurst despite the fact that I had beaten their team. Holden's PR machine went to work and I remember that they got the car down from Bathurst and we went to a big dealer launch at the Southern Cross Hotel in Melbourne and I had to drive the car into the auditorium and be with the dealers who I knew from my previous six years with HDT. From that point the car flew across to NZ to do a few races there. It was great fun. And from there I flew directly from NZ to South Africa where I went to Johannesburg to buy a BMW racing car. The whole idea was to take that racing car overseas and race it there under 'Team Australia'. It was terrific, we brought the car and that really served to break the ties with Gown Hindaugh, much

as they were fantastic guys. They had run out of money so I guessed it was simply time to move on and to pursue some of these international dreams we have as kids. So we prepared the BMW in Melbourne with the help of friends, family and people like that, and sent the car overseas. At this point I contacted Brian Muir to become a co-driver and we found that to make ends meet we needed to get a little bit of sponsorship here and there. We needed some one else to get in there to pay some bills and that is where John Claude Aubrier came in. Of course at this time it was time to look at forming our own racing team so my brother Phil and I got together and we came up with Team Brock which meant that yep! We built yet another L34 Torana and we put it together and went out there and went racing. The same guys who had worked for us at Gown Hindaugh came along and I think Garnet Bateson was a new addition to the team too.

It was great. A bunch of guys in a little factory out there in Bundoora. A few guys pitching in, Bob Buck and a few others. Really we just put a car together and went out on the track. This occurred while the BMW deal was still happening and preparing for that mid year excursion overseas. We had races to run in Melbourne and I will never forget getting that L34 on the track for the first time. I brought a second-hand car to drive, a road car, and we turned it into a race car. Slipped the engine out and we sort of tuned it up a bit and we put a cam in it and stuff like that. We actually went to Sandown for our debut race. We hadn't run the car before and started it up the night before in the court where the factory was set. We went to Sandown where I missed practice because we were running too late. So I had to start from the back of the grid on Sunday morning, so there we were at a round of the Australian Touring Car Championship and Frank Gardener was driving the old L34 Torana I had driven at Gown Hindaugh, Colin Bond, John Harvey, Bobby Morris and I suppose Alan Grice and there I was from the back of the grid.

Opposite – Peter in deep discussion with a passing fan at the launch of Team Brock Mark I.

Above – Parked at Brock's Big Day Out, Team Brock Mark II.

| Peter Brock in the L34.

Guess what? I actually hit the front before the race had finished but it coughed and spluttered right near the end of the race because we were using the standard Holden fuel tank, it wasn't big enough. So I didn't win the first race but I think I got second or so, you know it was a pretty good effort. We were all rapt.

How good was this! This car, first up has gone out there and gone real well, so for the next race you can imagine, we were thinking, what do we have to do to get through the same distance without the dramas. I think they were 40 lappers those races, a hell of a long distance. So what we did was to get the fuel tank and we blew it up with compressed air. We just turned the compressor on and blasted about 100 psi in the thing and bowed it out a bit like a balloon, and then away we went again. Filled it up with petrol and went

out there again for the next heat and won it, no problem! So it was a hell of a good debut for a new racing team, there is no doubt about that, and don't ask me how this can happen, that you can build a car straight off a shelf like that and bed the brakes in during the race. It is pretty weird but it happened. I guess a lot of people thought it was the result of a lot of secret testing and stuff. You could be forgiven as a motor racing person to think like that, but the truth is that the car went out there first time on the Sunday morning. To leave the pits and line up on the back of the grid at Sandown for the Australian Touring Car Championship and win a heat of the race. I wish I could say that motor racing is always like that but that is not the way motor racing usually unfolds."

Peter Brock

"**There were many expressions of interest** by people to find ways to harness his incredible ability and pulling power. Several such offers initially promised great things but resulted in severe disappointment. Peter understood that he was merely being used as a 'face' with little consideration being given to his extensive knowledge and ability to inspire teams. This disillusionment led to the reinvention of Team Brock in 2003, this time involving Jamie and Peter. Ross Palmer was setting up the Pro Car Series and saw Peter and James as a means to attracting other competitors and giving the formula credibility. There was also a need to provide up-and-coming drivers with a valuable experience.

Peter was approached by an 'investor' from New Zealand who wanted to fund the team with an enormous amount of money so that Team Brock could become the training ground for young enthusiasts who did not have the funding to get into the sport. It was to become a 'school' for potential mechanics, sports management people and drivers alike. Despite ongoing promises of the money being deposited into the account, it never appeared. Peter's trust in other people's honesty was once again severely tested. He invested large sums of personal money into the development of the team in preparation for the 'investment' which never appeared. This severely compromised Peter's finances and his faith in people.

There is no doubt that Peter was a great ideas man, a man of principle, a fantastic salesman and a charismatic leader. He was also without peer in his chosen sport, but he was incredibly trusting, which did nothing to ensure his ongoing success in the cut-and-thrust of the business world. This spelt the end of Team Brock."

Beverley Brock

Top – Peter Brock in Team Brock uniform.

Bottom – Peter, Jamie and Craig Baird at Clipsal, launching Team Brock Mark II.

Peter Brock in Team Brock uniform.
Opposite – Peter on the Goodwood track. (Photo provided by Peter and Sandy Champion)

"The Goodwood Festival of Speed is renowned as one of the premier motoring events in the world. It is held in the superb grounds of Goodwood house, a mere 60 miles from London. There is even an aerodrome on the property that caters for small planes and helicopters. So this is undoubtedly a paradise for any lover of fine vehicles or petrol head of any variety, and is seen as the largest motoring garden party in the world. It has been running since 1993.

The tens of thousands who flock to the festival each summer revel in the sight of the most superb collection of fine machinery the world has produced. Depending on the theme, visitors can feast their eyes on anything from Formula 1 cars to 200 MPH Supercars, Classic Rally cars, Steam Powered 19 Century Classics, 3000BHP Fuel Dragsters, and every superb road vehicle manufactured anywhere in the world.

Every car on display, right through to those participating in the annual hill climb, must be in their original livery and condition. The drivers invited are the most outstanding of their era. Each considers it a fantastic honour to be invited.

In 2005, Peter was invited along with Peter and Sandy Champion to run the famous 05 Big Banger at the festival. It was a dream invitation rarely extended to Australian cars and drivers.

The whole event was an amazing success. The car performed well and attracted enormous attention. The resonating roar of a V8 creates quite a stir in European circles and Peter proved to be a huge draw with the crowds. The chance to mix with the world's best in motor sport and enjoy such a spectacle was a pinnacle. He had already been voted 14 in the top 20 of the world's best ever drivers and had been elected the second best touring car driver in the world, so he was well known to the crowd, many of whom were regular watchers of Bathurst.

Such was the success of Peter's presence at the event that he was invited back with the early model Holden especially prepared and funded by his friend and supporter, Phil Munday. Once again the turnout and impact of Peter's run at the festival was fantastic. It was the last time he would drive a car on a race track. Immediately following his return to Australia, he was to head to Western Australia to run in the fateful rally that claimed his life."

Beverley Brock

| Phil Munday and Peter at Goodwood.

"Back in 2005, PB and I were talking about Goodwood and what a great thing it would be to take the Holden 48-215 and race it there. As I said to PB, 'The only thing is that we don't have a 48-215 race car!'

'Let's build one,' he says.

So after some discussion we put together a plan on how we would go about it and what we needed to do. First thing was to get an understanding on what type of spec the car was to be built on. This was left to Bob Harborough, who had a contact in England. Some time passed and one night we went out for PB's birthday in Hurstbridge in February and Peter said, 'I have something to show you.'

We went out to his car and he opened the tailgate and pulled out a piece of black cardboard rolled up, and said, 'Look at this, this is what the 48-2115 will look like.' It was a painting that Peter had done himself of what he had in mind. 'We should go ahead and build it,' he said. I asked him how long we had before we had to have the car in England. He said, 'On the water by the end of June!'

'Wow, this is not long to build a race car,' said I. PB handed me the painting and said, 'Happy Birthday' and, 'now we had better get on with the build, and soon.'

From that night onwards it was full-on, every moment of working with Peter was not all that easy (but was very exciting) as he would run ahead with the plans and moved very quickly with the build. PB organised a lot of his friends from the early HDT days, including Ian Tate, 'engine builder', Geoff Hall, 'brakes man' etc. The progress on the car was pushing ahead at full steam until one day I happened to ask PB, 'Have you got the invitation from the Lord Earl of March?' PB's reply was, 'No, not yet, but don't worry, it will come.' This was a little alarming to me as here we were building this car and we didn't as yet have the invitation?

But we pressed on until one day in early June 2006, we were ready to have our first 'shake down' at Calder Park. It was a very cold Wednesday and out we went. The car performed extremely well and after a full day out we had decided what changes were needed. So back to the factory to make the changes.

PB at Calder Park raceway for the first 'shake down'.
(Photo supplied by Phil Munday)

Phil Munday and Peter Brock checking out the 48-215 race-car engine. (Photo supplied by Phil Munday)

Opposite – Peter Brock in the Big Banger at Goodwood 2005.

A few days later I received the invitation from the Lord Earl of March. I was so excited that all of this work was now coming to fruition and rang PB to tell him the news. All he said was, 'I knew it would come sooner or later.' But I knew he was excited as well. All the late nights and long days now seemed worthwhile. One more test at Calder Park and then the car went into a container for a 6-week trip to England.

We arrived in England on 28th August 2006 and headed straight off to Goodwood to see if the car was there. It was not! I waited for Peter to turn up at the track and he was as shocked as I. There followed many frantic phone calls and finally it showed up on the back of a tow truck. What a relief! All that way from home and it would seem we had no control. So, Thursday was D-day for everyone to set up in their pit garages. So many people came to our garage and were looking at the 49 series (or fx as it is commonly known). The English could not believe it was so big. Some were saying that it looked like an oversized Morris Minor.

Friday was the first time out on the track. Wow, how good did it go? And the sound! People were running up to the fence around the track to see it go past them. It was great!!!

Saturday was the big race... First race in the St Marys trophy race. Peter was 5th on the grid. A big smile on his face. Thumbs up as the cars took off for their warm-up lap. It was raining and slightly foggy. PB came around the track to the start line. I was up in a tree to get a better look at the start. All lined up, engines roaring, ready for the drop of the flag. PB looks up, gives the thumbs up and the flag drops. Off they go into the first corner, sideways in the wet. The crowd are up on their feet. What an experience! Twelve laps after zig zagging through the other cars, mostly sideways in the wet, he finishes 4th. Afterwards, in our debriefing, we realised that the car had an oil pressure problem. This meant that there would be no Sunday race.

Monday morning about 7am, my phone rang and it's PB with the news that we'd won the Spirit of Goodwood trophy. So we met at the track at around 9.30am and caught up with the organiser of the event who told us that the Lord Earl of March would like to invite us to lunch and present us with the trophy, which he did. We had a fabulous time with him and his family.

After lunch, we said our farewells and hugs... Little did I know that this would be the last time I would ever see Peter Brock."

Phil Munday
(Owner of Munday's Panel Repair Shop & Property Developer)

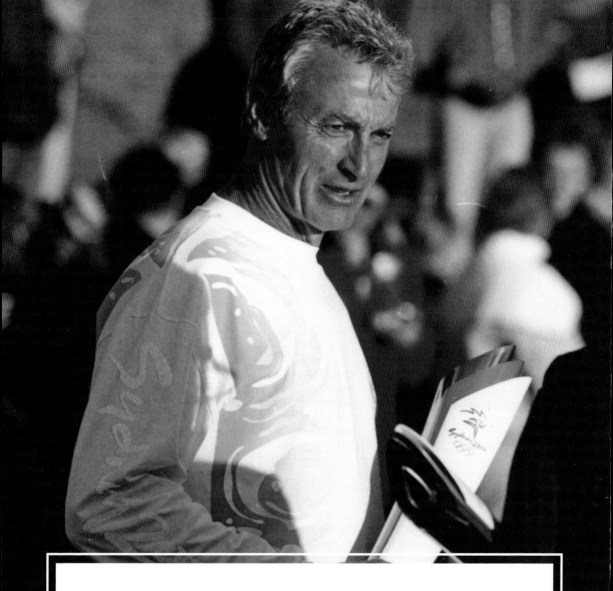

CHAPTER NINE

OLYMPICS EXPERIENCE

"To be given the opportunity to mentor the cream of the athletes is an incredible honour – and front row seats, awesome."

"Peter had become known in the general sporting community as a sportsman of the highest integrity who focused on his own performance rather than that of his competitors. He was also vocal on the need to give your very best rather than to win at any cost.

Peter was approached by the organisers of the Sydney Olympics for the role of an Athlete Liaison Officer, which meant that he would mentor and support athletes, who in turn could talk about their concerns with someone who understood the pressures of elite sport.

Generally, people placed in these positions were ex Olympians and there had never been any previous motor sport competitors involved.

Peter Brock having a great time at the 2000 Olympics.
Opposite – No better man to carry the torch.

For Peter, this was an amazing opportunity and a tremendous accolade. He had a wisdom that had admittedly taken some years to arise. I guess that is the advantage of being able to compete at the top level of a sport for so many years. In most sports, athletes have passed their peak before they have had a chance to mature.

Here was an opportunity he could only have dreamt of previously. He had access to the best seats in the house, the ear of the best athletes Australia had to offer, and got to share ideas and conversations with the likes of Herb Elliott and John Coates.

Over the following pages is a sample of how he spoke to the athletes and a few of his favourite memories.

Beverley Brock

"In life you get to challenge yourself

and I am a firm believer that the way that you are is a firm result of all of the experiences that you have had. It has made you who you are. You are the sum total. Your thought, your belief system of what you have taken on board as being good, bad or indifferent or whatever. In fact, everything that has ever happened right now, at this point in time has shaped you to be who you are. You have challenged yourself to do something which is extraordinary, and whether you have seen it that way or not, the fact is you have chosen that training regime to get yourself here into the Olympics. You sit here right here and now to say I am going to put myself out there. Now one part of you is saying I don't really want to do that and another part of you is exhilarated by it. Another part of you might say:

'But what if I fail?'

You start concentrating on all of these different things. Now what this is all about is controlling your thoughts, mental discipline. Stopping your mind running rampant and creating all sorts of unreasonable and unrealistic situations. Stop yourself from doing that by simply reigning your mind in. The moment you see your mind doing that, you stop it. The moment you find yourself getting involved in some huge emotional drama over there, stop it because you have got to pat yourself on the back for challenging yourself. Not too many people do. Most people would prefer the easy way out. They sit back there and simply let life be safe. You have chosen not to do this. So that means that you may well finish up going through some emotional highs and lows, it is up to you.

All you know is you are going to tell yourself that the choices you have made were the fastest growth curve you could possibly put yourself through as an individual character development.

So, pat yourself on the back. Now if you fail, you need to look at what were your expectations. The only expectations you should ever have is that you are going to give it your best shot. Now if you are silly enough to go out on the booze two nights beforehand or you go and eat the wrong foods or you go and do something which is going to be debilitating, such as a huge argument, some stressed out drama with someone around you so that you are a mess. Well at the end of the day, you have to sit back and say, 'I didn't give it my best shot. I knew those things were dumb, I knew those things weren't the right thing to do and therefore I shot myself in the foot. I actually decided that I wasn't quite ready for it.

Are you ready for it?

Now if you are going to go out there and give it your best shot, and you have taken care of all of those things beforehand, I can't see how you can have any regrets. You can't be feeling low afterwards because you have done everything that is humanly possible and therefore you have got to forgive yourself for not achieving what everyone else thought you should have achieved. On this day that is all you can do. You gave it your best shot, this is what you achieved, walk away and have a clear conscience. Look at yourself in the mirror each morning and acknowledge that, that is the way it worked out for you.

As I keep on saying, you are not going to win every time you walk out there. That is not what life is all about. It is unrealistic. Sometimes it is someone else's turn. It is as simple as that. They are all striving for the same things in life as you. You can't have 10 people in the same car going through the same corner at Bathurst. They all want to go through first. They are all visualising it, all training for it and all planning for it but it ain't going to happen. So you have got to have this idea in your mind that 'Hey, I am going to go out there and have a red hot go!'

PB handing the Olympic torch to Craig Lowndes at Bathurst.

Happy snaps with Patrick Johnson and Kyle Vander Kuyp; *trying his prowess with paralympians; and with Jelena Dokic.*

There are many highlights that stick in my mind from the Olympics. There was a basketball game. I think it was against the Lithuanians, and it was a magic night. We walked out of the stadium and we were singing. We had a group of Aussies that hung around us. I think Laurie Lawrence was with us and I got involved with sneaking people in as well. We might have had 40 passes, we would plead for passes from SOCOG and I would have my pass in my pocket and I would say to everyone, come on just come with me. One night I had 300-odd athletes and they were all singing out that Brocky had the passes, come on we can all get in, and I would simply wave them all in. 'Hey look at this,' and in we would go with the Aussies all in war paint. It happened a few times. I would negotiate with them, though, earlier on (the venue management) and some of those nights were magic because our group would come in there, the team would come out and they would turn around and see all their mates, 300 Aussies just ga-ga. It was just fantastic, magic, electric.

The coaches had asked me to have a word with Grant Hackett prior to the competition because he had been going lousy in the shorter races and everyone had been saying that he had some sort of physical disability, some sort of crook gut or the like.

The volunteers were sensational. They had smuggled Grant's folks in to talk to him before the event. I had been focusing very much on just doing what we were meant to be doing. I had said to him just get in that pool and swim, get into the rhythm of doing it. My analogy to all of them was, individually and collectively, was... Ok. At the start of Bathurst, you drop the clutch and get off the mark, get to the first corner and go up the next straight, into the right hander and go to the top of the mountain and you are looking good. Get into the next corner, and the next. Get all of your braking points right. Go down conrod, finish off the first lap, looking good, now just do it another 160 times. That is it! You can't get ahead of yourself. This business of seeing yourself on the dais is nuts. You are jumping ahead of the now moment. The now moment is all that matters because how you are in the now moment controls your future. So don't live in your future because it is just not the way it works out.

So to be there as a part of the support amongst the swimming group at pool side, to watch that event unfold and to have felt so personally involved in the whole thing, the way it was working out, was just magic. There were a number of nights like that. I remember being out with the bike riders in the velodrome and I thought that Garry Niewand was just fantastic. He knew he had to take the lead a long way from home and knew he couldn't take the draft because the other guys were going to push him wide, they were going to chop him up. So he said I have got to take the lead early and just go like the wind and he almost got there... He was one of the greatest athletes in the team. He was tough mentally and had already achieved a lot.

On the night of Cathy's race we had to come across from the beach where the beach volleyballers had won. We had spent some time with them going to training and dinners with them so really knew them by this time. I had spent the day in the stands whipping up the crowds for their match. I remember standing over the other side at the beach court and had to go and find Dawn Fraser and tell her I needed a lift back to the athletic stadium. The guy that was the Lord Mayor of Sydney came out and we all got a lift back to the Olympic stands. We had so many passes. We had photocopied passes to stick on top of the original passes so it looked like you were an athlete. Anyway we had hundreds coming, we just rolled in and everyone at the gate knew it was a scam and they just rolled their eyes. We had Steve Waugh with us and we parked ourselves in the athletes stand. Steve was just in civvies and I pulled a team jacket out of my back pack for him to put on but he wouldn't do it because he wasn't a member of the team. We got him in anyway.

It was, well, excellent. I saw quite a bit of the athletics and some of our guys were just crushed because they didn't do as well as they thought they should have. Those kids were just fantastic. Tamsyn Lewis was just great, as was Jana Pittman. I said to her that she ran like an Ethiopian. She would just go. She was concerned as she had lost count of her steps between the hurdles and she asked me what advice I had for her. I told her it was simple, I said she had obviously been involved in athletics since she was a kid, which she agreed to. So I said it was just like that. Remember when you were a kid and just be a kid and learn to count again. She just laughed. I said, 'Have no limits in your mind as to what you can do. You will get people in your ear telling you, you can't run fast because it is too windy, or the track conditions are too cold and your muscles will tense up. Just get out there and run!'"

Peter Brock

Peter Brock's collection of happy snaps from the Sydney Olympics, taken with his own camera (which he'd palm off to the nearest passerby).

Opposite – On the starting grid with Laurie Lawrence.

"I've never been a car racing nut, frankly find it difficult to even distinguish one car from another. Well all that was to change in Sydney 2000!

The city was buzzing with Olympic fever and I was to live in the village with a number of Australian sporting identities hand-picked by the great Herb Elliott and charged with:

'Creating an atmosphere to relax unite and inspire our Australian Olympic team.'

There I met PB, one Peter Brock, motor-racing legend!

I was amazed at his communication skills. I became an immediate friend and fan transfixed by his regal carriage, infectious smile, serious no-nonsense business-like approach to sport and life.

Young and old athletes alike would gather round PB for a regular dose of 'Brocksay' interspersed with stories from his famous racing career.

Whether it be Olympic Champion Grant Hackett or some young athlete new to the Olympics Brocky always had time to sit down, relax with them, and give them multiple reasons why they were going to perform at their very best.

Always positive, he created a great impression on all team members. So popular was he that he was invited back to perform the same duties in Athens where I was his roommate. He was always up early exercising before taking off for his daily appointments. We spent many late nights and early mornings solving the problems of the world and discussing in detail how we could assist the athletes without interfering with the coaches.

London will be a duller place without my old roommate, but as I watch, cheer and communicate with Olympians past and future I know PB will be looking over my shoulder to whisper a little 'Brocksay'.

Laurie Lawrence
(Swimming coach and legend)

CHAPTER TEN

AWARDS & ACCOLADES

"Awards were a little humbling for me personally. My kids didn't even know that I had won the Order of Australia because it wasn't something we ever talked about."

To

PETER GEOFFREY BROCK

Greeting

*W*HEREAS *Her Majesty Queen Elizabeth The Second, Queen of Australia, has instituted an Australian medal to commemorate the centenary of federation of Australia; I DO by this warrant award you the Centenary Medal.*

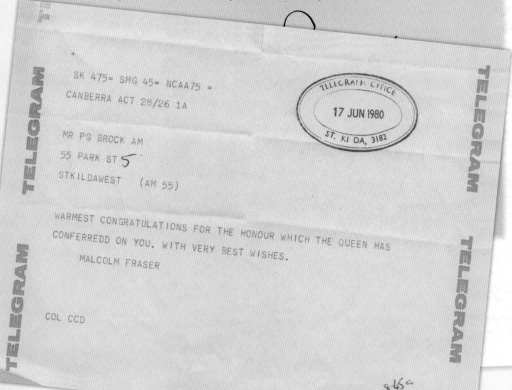

SK 475= SMG 45= NCAA75 =
CANBERRA ACT 28/26 1A

TELEGRAPH OFFICE
17 JUN 1980
ST. KILDA, 3182

MR PG BROCK AM
55 PARK ST 5
STKILDAWEST   (AM 55)

WARMEST CONGRATULATIONS FOR THE HONOUR WHICH THE QUEEN HAS
CONFERREDD ON YOU. WITH VERY BEST WISHES.
     MALCOLM FRASER

COL CCD

"Peter was somewhat cavalier about recognition although he acknowledged that it could be 'useful' when seeking sponsorship.

1980 – Peter was honoured as a Member of the General Division of the Order of Australia for his services to motor sport. Peter felt humbled by the award and duly tucked it away in a cupboard.

| *Bev and PB at a Sportsman of the Year Award dinner.*

1984 – Peter received the Sports Australia Award for Outstanding Performance seeing he had won virtually everything it was possible to win that year.

1986 – Peter was crowned King of Moomba in May that year which gave him the opportunity to share the carnival with his kids, which gave him great delight. He was the first King to be introduced to the Queen of England who happened to be in Australia at the time. Special permission had to be sought in order for him to wear his 'cloth' crown in her Majesty's presence!

1997 – Peter was inducted into the Australian Hall of Fame along with the likes of Ron Barassi, Hayley Lewis and David Campese.

1998 – Peter was runner-up to Cathy Freeman as Australian of the Year.

2000 – Peter was awarded the Australian Sports Medal. This award was introduced in 1999 to recognise the sporting achievements of Australians who have made this country a nation of sporting excellence.

2001 – Peter was honored with the Prime Minister's Centenary Medal for services to the Community. He was also an Ambassador for Australia Day.

Peter Brock Award

Est. 2011

In honour of motor sport legend, the late Peter Brock AM,
this award recognises outstanding driver ability
and commitment to the positive endorsement of motor sport
within the greater community.

The Peter Brock Medal, designed by the Brock family and awarded to the most promising young driver each year. The inaugural winner was a posthumous presentation to Jason Richards. Jason was told of his award shortly before his death.

While honoured by these awards, Peter made virtually no reference to them throughout his life unless required for reasons of protocol. The awards were carefully stored in an insulated shipping container, to prevent Peter from giving them away if he felt they would give someone pleasure or they could be used to raise funds for charity. In order to protect these for posterity, it became necessary to hide them from him. His gloves, driving suits, helmets and paintings would be given away to those who merely asked."

Beverley Brock

"Peter wasn't great at surprises, but with due

consideration between Colleen Adamson, his personal and commercial manager, and myself, we felt that *This is Your Life* was too good an opportunity to pass up. To get Peter completely thrown off track, the producers decided that Peter was to believe he was doing an interview that would involve him completing a tandem sky jump with a landing at Albert Park. That concept was testosterone-driven enough to excite him, and excite him it did. Unfortunately, the day was too windy and the jump was impossible, so with frantic last minute adjustments he had to arrive at the interview point by more conventional means. The site of the interview had been set up as a vintage Mobil service station which provided the initial surprise for the day.

Meanwhile. the rest of the family – including our latest litter of border collie pups – were spirited away to the studios without him being aware that anything unusual was occurring. The surprise element gives the show its buzz and a great deal of effort had been put into getting the invited guests from overseas, interstate and from the suburbs together without word getting out. There were many that Peter had not seen for some years. It was exciting and nerve-wracking not quite knowing how he was going to respond to it all. He was known to occasionally have an outburst of irritation when the unexpected happened so it was like treading on egg shells for the weeks leading up to the big day.

The evening was superb, exhilarating and a total success. Peter felt absolutely honoured and was amazed by the effort that had been put into every aspect of the show. Even those sections that could have been controversial went down well. The after-party following the filming – which was attended by invited guests consisting of family, long-lost friends and associates who had been sworn to secrecy – was a night to remember.

It left us all with a new found respect for the production and research team that create a night of magic for those fortunate few who get to experience a review of their extraordinary lives in this manner."

Beverley Brock

Top right – Mike Munro surprising Peter Brock.
Above – Peter Brock (thankfully) enjoying the surprise.
Opposite – The special guests of the show.

PB getting set to drop the chequered flag at the
Australian Grand Prix. (With thanks to the AGP)

"As Australians we are all too ready to see ourselves as lesser than, not quite up to the mark, and we readily accept that if a sporting event is from a famous overseas venue, it's got to be good.

I've been doing a lot of travelling lately putting together a new TV show, and nothing gets clearer in your mind than to see for yourself those cities, the venues and the local people firsthand.

Invariably the conversation gets around to Melbourne and our sporting fame. As one guy in Cuba said, 'We hear a lot about you Aussies, you're making a lot of noise for only 17 million.'

The Grand Prix is really focussing attention on Melbourne and I wonder just how much recognition there would be without it. No doubt the Olympics, the Opera House and the Harbour Bridge all work well for Sydney. Like it or not, most people tend to equate these things with what this country has to offer. The Grand Prix is helping people realise that 'Yes, Melbourne, the city with the F1 race...!'

Since I retired late last year, I've been able to get a bit more involved with the AGP. The size and magnitude of the event and the organisational effort it takes to make it work smoothly is by any estimation, huge. The AGP is the single biggest annual sporting event in Australia, and to be a part of it is an enormous honour. To have been elected to join the Board makes me feel incredibly privileged.

This year they also asked if I'd mind if they named one of the new spectator mounds 'Brocky's Hill'. I drove around, had a look at the site, asked some questions about the proximity of the high resolution video screen, the thoroughfares and other attractions and said a resounding 'Yes!' This could be one of the best general admission viewing areas, and I'll be calling by to say 'hi' and sign a few things over the GP meeting.

Later the powers that be asked if I would like to drop the chequered flag on the winner of the race. My initial response was sure, that will mean I will get a pit pass and get even closer to the action. Then the realisation hit, 350 million people will see me do my thing, so I've been sort of practicing out here on the farm. I'm trying for a unique style, part AFL umpy, part Glen Dix, the legendary motor race flaggie. The pressure's on, I guess, to add my part to showcase Melbourne's Albert Park, as the most beautiful race track and to do whatever I can to help once again make it the best GP in the world.

The AFL Grand Final and the Melbourne Cup are great traditional Melbourne events; however the Grand Prix is on a bigger scale. I know the other events get considerable overseas exposure but the Grand Prix is a serious mainstream event."

Peter Brock

| PB signing posters at the Australian Grand Prix.

Practice makes perfect as PB drops the chequered flag on the winner of the Australian Grand Prix. (With thanks to the AGP)

"Champions, regardless of the sport, share a common trait: the ability to focus their whole being on an objective. It's less common to find champions who are willing to use that intensity to help others achieve their goals. Peter Brock was that kind of man.

And he had another quality which, combined with the first two, made him so formidable: he had an unquenchable optimism. With Peter, the glass was always half full, even when, from where you stood, it looked rather empty.

Focus, intensity, optimism. These were the tools that Peter used to turn ideas into reality.

It was a 'no-brainer' to ask Peter to join the board of the Australian Grand Prix Corporation and he served from 1998 until his fatal accident in 2006. He was full of ideas and always ready to help, giving both his time and his legendary status in support of the Formula 1 event. One of the favourite viewing areas on the Albert Park circuit was named after him. Brocky's Hill was – and still is – the target for a stampede of spectators when the gates open each day during the Grand Prix. He always made a point of going there to spend time with other motor sport fans.

But, of course, he couldn't only be a spectator. In 1996 he won a V8 race at the Grand Prix and in 2000 went head to head with his old adversary Alan Moffat during the event, driving a Torana XU-1 against Moffat's Falcon GTHO Phase 3 – cars in which they raced each other at Bathurst in 1972.

In 1998 we gave Peter the honour of waving the chequered flag to end that year's Formula 1 race. Mika Hakkinen won, followed closely by his McLaren teammate David Coulthard in second. I recall thinking at the time, as millions of people watched around the world, that we couldn't have had a better ambassador for motor sport in Australia. That is how I remember Peter Brock.

I am proud to say he was my friend."

Ronald Walker

AC CBE, Chairman, Australian Grand Prix Corporation

A collage of photos, awards, certificates and congratulatory letters from *various distinguished people.*

PRIME MINISTER
CANBERRA

9 April 2003

C 3099

...ulate you on being approved for the award of the
...al by the Governor-General. Nominations for the medal were
...mmonwealth, State and Territory governments and
...by the independent Council for the Centenary Medal.

...ve Australian commemorative medal marks the achievements at
...ement of a new century of a Australian society. Australia is
...including your contribution to Australian society. Australia is
...it has many outstanding people who have helped make our country
...er world a better place.

...Medal in the near

...ents will be made for you to

...ncerely,

(John Howard)

To **PETER GEOFFREY BROCK** Greeting

WHEREAS Her Majesty Queen Elizabeth The Second,
Queen of Australia, has instituted an Australian medal,
to commemorate the centenary of federation of Australia;
I DO by this warrant award you the Centenary Medal.

By His Excellency's Command

Governor-General of the
Commonwealth of Australia

Prime Minister

COPPER
BLUEY ™
-a- Cop

Certificate of Appreciation

Presented to

PETER BROCK

of

MOBIL HOLDEN RACING TEAM

*in grateful recognition of your
generous support to the*

1997 Crop-a-Cop Campaign

BRETT FLORENCE
SENIOR CONSTABLE 27598

16TH of AUGUST, 1997

MINISTER FOR NATIONAL DEVELOPMENT AND ENERGY

LEADER OF THE GOVERNMENT IN THE SENATE

PARLIAMENT HOUSE
CANBERRA A.C.T.

P. G. Brock, AM
...rk Street,
...LDA WEST   VIC   3182

Dear Mr. Brock,

I was personally very pleased to see in the ...
Birthday List that you had been awarded the h...
honour of A.M. for your contribution to the s...
motor racing in Australia.

You are a recognised leader in your chosen fie...
you merit this significant award.

Please accept my warm congratulations and goo...

Yours sincerely,

PARLIAMENT OF AUSTRALIA · THE SENATE

SENATOR L.W. NEAL BA., BEd.,
COMMONWEALTH PARLIAMENT OFFICES,
400 FLINDERS STREET,
MELBOURNE VICTORIA 3000
(03) 622921
6511

23 June 1980

Dear Mr Brock,

I was happy to see that on the Queen's
Birthday Weekend, public recognition was given to
you for a life of achievement and service to the
Community.

Decorations such as yours are only earned
by a small section of the Community, thus making
this award a special event in the life of the
Nation, Yourself and Family.

Please accept my hearty congratulations
on this recognition, and all that it conveys
concerning Yourself.

All thinking Australian Citizens are
proud of You!

Best wishes,

Yours sincerely,

Laurie Neal

(L.W. NEAL)
Senator for Victoria

Mr P.G. Brock, A.M.,
55 Park Street,
ST KILDA WEST   3182

Dear Mr Brock,

I am writing to congratulate y
appointment as a Member of the Order of A

Your contribution to Motor Rac
been significant and as Federal Minister
responsible for Sport and Recreation, I am
that it has been recognised in this way.

Yours sincerely

R.J. Ellicott
Minister for Home Aff

.G. Brock, A.M.,
rk Street,
ILDA WEST, VIC. 3182

SPORTSMEN

SPORT AUSTRALIA AWARDS
ertificate of Outstanding Performance

PETER BROCK

1984 YEAR OF THE YEAR

SPORT

Executive Director

PRIME MINISTER
CANBERRA

24.Feb.95 12:11 No.005 P.01

Mr Peter Brock
C/- Mike Raymond
Seven Network Motorsport
Television Centre
EPPING NSW 2121

Dear Mr Brock

It gives me great pleasure to join the motor racing industry today in extending to you
my best wishes on your 50th birthday.

Celebrating this milestone behind the wheel while competing in the second round of the
Shell Australian touring car championship is typical of the Brock legend.

Congratulations,

P J KEATING

THE ORDER OF AUSTRALIA

To PETER GEOFFRE

Whereas with the approval of
The Second Queen of Australia and S
I have been pleased to appoint you to be a
of the Order of Australia.
I DO by these Presents appoint y
General Division of the said Order and i
dignity of such appointment together with
and all privileges thereunto appertaining.
GIVEN at Government House, C
Order of Australia this fourteenth day of Jo

By His Excelle

Secretary of the Order

Peter Brock receiving his Medal of the Order of Australia from Governor General, Sir Zelman Cowen in 1980.

CHAPTER ELEVEN

LIFELONG PASSIONS

*"I played centre half-forward, or half-forward flank for Diamond Creek.
That is more or less just down the road. I loved playing footy.
I was pretty good at it too."*

"In the heyday of HDT, Peter commissioned a 40-foot boat to be built by his mate John Farrell. Peter would occasionally join John and his mates for a fishing trip to Exmouth in the North West. On one such occasion, they had just thrown in their lines early in the morning when Peter hooked a sizeable catch. He was only using a light line which made landing the fish a drawn-out affair. After about an hour and a half, Peter finally landed a

Giant Trevally and casually threw it on the deck. He was not an expert on sea creatures or fishing competitions and simply left the fish on the deck throughout the remainder of the day.

When the boats returned to the wharf with the setting sun, the diehards at the weigh-in expressed great excitement on seeing the poor fish which had, by this time, dehydrated somewhat throughout the day. It turned out to be a world record catch by a substantial amount on that line strength. The shock of killing something so amazing caused PB to give up fishing forever."

Beverley Brock

Top – The new Broadbill in full flight.

Above – Peter and Bev towing the brand new Broadbill behind the Commodore Wagon. It had been delivered at Bathurst and had to be towed to Melbourne.

Opposite – Peter at the weigh in with his record-breaking trevally in 1981.

PB battling to land the 37.53kg trevally.

None

"The Brock family and Collingwood are synonymous!

You are battling to be a member of the family if your loyalties happen to lie elsewhere.

Peter would play kick-to-kick with his Uncle Sandy for hours at the farm. The family used to go to the VFL games whenever possible to watch their beloved 'Pies'. If it meant that the boys would climb through fences or jump on top of shed roofs so that they could see a game for nothing, so be it.

He was absolutely dedicated to the Mighty Pies and the opportunity to participate in the era of the 'New Magpies' was too big to pass up. Ranald McDonald (President of Collingwood 1982–86) became a close friend and Peter was elected a member of the board. To say he was ecstatic is an understatement. It was, however, to be a short stay as they all knew that the demands of his career and public life left little time for anything else.

It was also about this time that Peter became closely involved in negotiating details around Peter Daicos and the determination to keep him at the team. The 'magician' could not be allowed to fall into the hands of any opposing team. Peter's intense focus on this objective was not to be dismissed lightly. The daily intrigue became a challenge and a fascination that resulted in a close friendship with Daic's that lasted throughout Peter's life.

It was typical that the practice day for the Sandown 500 was on the same day as the preliminary finals for the footy. If Collingwood had made it that far, there was a regular update of the scores. Nothing would distract him from his race preparation except the mighty Pies.

Collingwood's incredible 1990 grand final win was as good as a personal win at Bathurst. Perhaps it was even better, because at that time Peter had won at the mountain nine times, where as his 'boys' had not seen a win for many years. However, as the race at Bathurst loomed on the immediate horizon, the celebrations that night were short and dry. He arrived home to a mass of banners, balloons and black and white decorations as the entire family knew just how much this meant to him.

Peter treasured very few possessions in his life as he was not a materialist. He did, however, own two jumpers once worn by Daic's. They were revered like little else that he owned."

Beverley Brock

Brock's bar at Mount Pleasant Rd, complete with a Magpies window and Collingwood port collection.

Opposite – Peter Brock beside the specially-made door he had commissioned for the old house. He personally built the window into cupboards he made in his Middle Park home.

"I played centre half-forward, or half- forward flank for Diamond Creek. That is more or less just down the road. I loved playing footy. I was pretty good at it too. At one point it was a toss-up between whether I would get into the VFL – as it was known then – or go motor racing. I was invited to train at Collingwood, because this was their recruiting area. I actually got pretty close to a career in footy.

However, at the age of 18 or 19, cars got to me. That was it. But I loved my footy. I still do and I follow it quite closely. I just found, as an individualist, playing in a team situation did not fully gratify me. I mean, as a player you might pull down a good mark, get back, set up a play, and boot it down the field to someone. You have done your bit, and everything is looking good, and then someone else stuffs it up. I just used to think, 'What the hell!'"

Peter Brock

Peter's Collingwood 'emblems' at home in Eltham.

"We drove our cars and chose Holdens because of him, pictures of

him adorned parts of rooms in family homes, sporting writers needed him and current drivers say he inspired them to take up the sport. He was fuelled and was fuelling his craft while forever being acknowledged as the 'KING' of Australian Motor Racing. The question I ask myself a lot is who could be considered our second best driver and how far away from Brocky is he – in my eyes, MILES AWAY!!!

I first met Peter Brock in 1983, spotting him at different times trying to be anonymous. He would stand at the back of crowds in our Collingwood Change rooms at games from time to time. I remember the buzz it would send through the rooms with us players, who would be well aware of his presence.

After being officially introduced to PB during '83, I remember starting to visit him at his North Melbourne workshop many times, at least once a week. Never in that time was I a burden to him, as he always made you feel that he was genuinely happy to see you there.

One of the things he loved to do was grab a footy and kick it around his workshop, or laneway out the back. I can recall many a time the ball landing on his works of art, modified Holden Commodores being transformed into a 'HDT Brock Special'. The glares his mechanics would give me or him, would have sat nicely on the face of some hardnosed, half-back flanker in any game of AFL Football.

His knowledge of football was very good, and I really enjoyed our chats after games, including his input into my goalkicking style and general football play. All jokes aside, he was up to speed with the game at that time.

The biggest thrills afforded to me occurred while being taken for drives around surrounding streets close to his workshop. He would take me for spins while hitting extraordinary speeds. I apologise for not being precise with what speed we exactly hit at times, as it is a little difficult when you have your eyes shut and that occurred frequently. Add to this the laps around the circuit at Sandown and you can understand why it was so easy to admire and appreciate his friendship.

The other thing I found with him is that he seemed to be a little child-like at times. I say this because he would get so excited about things in a game of football or with anything that was happening in his life, family and business – I loved these moments because he was so infectious with his passion for things and life. I remember someone once saying that you should never meet your heroes, as most of the time you come away a little sadder because of the experience, but I can honestly say that this was never the case with PB, he just made you feel so much better for the experience, making you look forward to the next get-together.

At times it's not what people say or do, but 'how they make you feel' – this was Peter Brock, who had that great ability to make you feel so good about yourself. He was a wonderful host and listener who let you hold court, he was always interested to hear your views on different matters and he was totally accessible to us all.

I am so much greater for having met and known Peter Brock – but more importantly to have said he was my friend."

Peter Daicos
Collingwood legend

Peter Brock and Peter Daicos after a lap at Sandown.

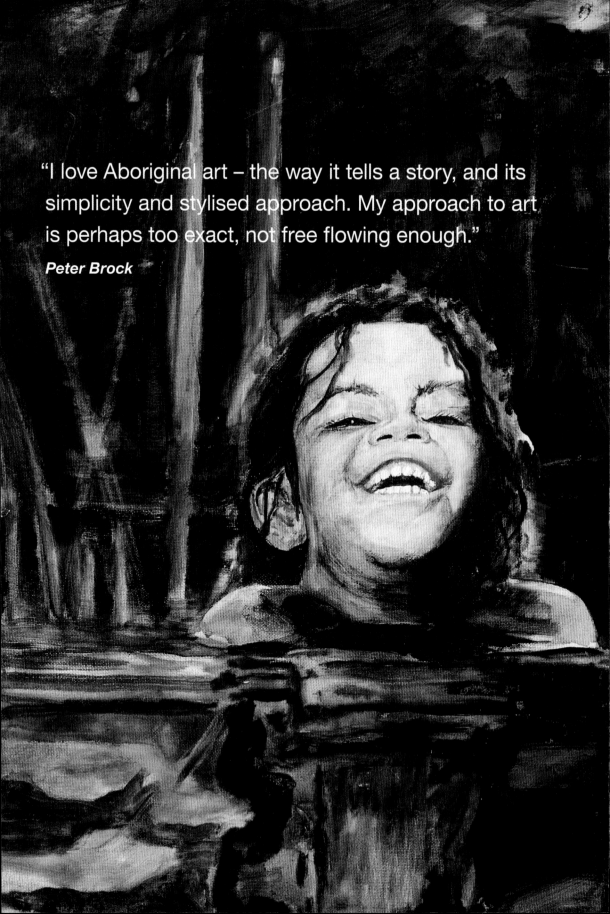

"I love Aboriginal art – the way it tells a story, and its simplicity and stylised approach. My approach to art is perhaps too exact, not free flowing enough."

Peter Brock

"From the time Peter could hold a pencil he would draw. It was one

of the rare occasions when he would be still, no matter what stage of life we are talking about. Initially, his drawings reflected his love of machinery. As he grew, so did his interests.

Peter was mates with the Jorgensen boys from Montsalvat, which even then was home for an eclectic and diverse group of artists. This period of time had such an impact on Peter that he wanted very much to create a similar environment on the farm in order to encourage young and developing artists who find it a struggle to support themselves.

The quality of the paper was not of any relevance to Peter and many of his sketches are found on partially used pieces of note paper, the inside covers of note books and the blank columns of magazines. The family found a trip to the art supplies stores provided a much appreciated gift for him whenever it was called for.

Drawing and painting soothed his soul. It gave him relaxation from an overactive mind. No matter how much work was done at the factory or on the farm, he was never satisfied. He would see further possibilities, so there was always more to do. But all of this changed when he started drawing or painting. Some article or view or face would catch his eye and get the same degree of focus as the road in front of him when behind the wheel of a car. Nothing could distract him; he would disappear down to where his glorious finches flitted amongst the trees and bushes, sketchbook in hand and lose himself in the moment.

The area that had once been his potting room for generating the many thousands of seedlings he grew to eventually cover huge areas of the farm gave way to a purpose-built mudbrick studio. Peter decided that it would be a fantastic project to give Jamie's mates to do. It was a part of 'learning' their craft. The studio became a collection of ideas and pieces contributed by the creative souls that he tended to draw around him.

Peter's sketch of a restless flycatcher and exquisite nest he found on the farm.

Opposite – His finest painting – copied from one of Peter McCanchie's photographs taken in the Northern Territory.

His many trips to Australia's Outback gave him a love of rich colours, so much so that he was determined to paint the house in those hues. He was away on a longer trip when the painting was being done. We had started to paint the outside walls and we all stood back and surveyed the result with horror. A joint family and tradesmen decision was made in his absence to abandon the colour choice as we knew we couldn't live with it. Numerous batches of colour were mixed and tried until we at last found one that we thought might be in his palette and that we could accept. Once the decision was reached, the painting progressed at a great rate and was almost complete when he returned. 'Not happy, Bevo!' was the response.

But the job was done, and the slightly ochre/pink was finally and begrudgingly accepted although not forgotten.

Many of Peter's finest works were produced to sell for charity auctions. So many requests were made for items to auction that it became difficult to keep up the supply. He would sit on the floor in the upstairs bedroom, the sun pouring in the window, and draw and paint the tree outside or the hillside or pond he could see. He would then add one of his early cars, complete with the correct number plate that he never forgot. That way he combined his two loves, nature and cars, and would feel complete satisfaction.

His best ever portrait was one done of a young Aboriginal child from a photo taken by Peter McConchie for one of his books that told the stories of the indigenous folk in Northern Australia.

There is little doubt that Peter could well have been content to paint his way through his retirement had it ever come to pass."

Beverley Brock

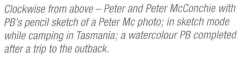

Clockwise from above – Peter and Peter McConchie with PB's pencil sketch of a Peter Mc photo; in sketch mode while camping in Tasmania; a watercolour PB completed after a trip to the outback.

Opposite – Peter's mudbrick studio built on the farm.

GEOFF, FATHER,
PA, DAD.

Left – Peter's portrait of his daughter, Alexandra (DD).

Above – Portrait of Geoff, Peter's dad, done for Father's Day.

Opposite – Self-portrait auctioned at the launch of the PBF, bought by Robert Shannon.

Pete Gosdon
Nov 97

Silver

30mm

170mm

Black
630mm

480mm

180
↓

20mm

60mm

17×8
with Bridgestone G111
(special package deal
via B.S. dealers)

PB's natural flair for art also enabled him to communicate effectively in the workshop, and he did all the technical drawings for his ideas, prototypes and modifications. He kept many and a few are shown here.

Roof

V8 BRutes

47 POOLRITE SMART SYSTEMS ROH

HOLDEN

Gecko Branle

armor all

Branle

Branle

18×8 as seen at Monaro performance centre

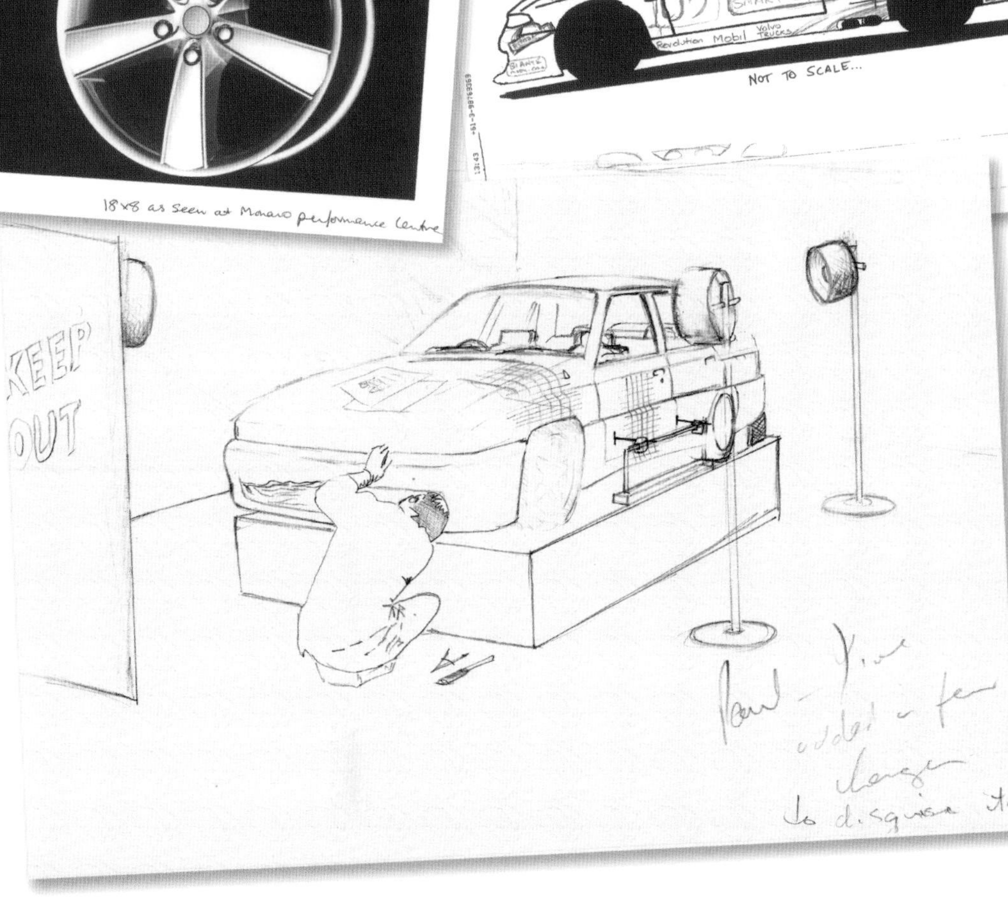

BRIDGESTONE 05 POOLRITE SMART SYS ROH
Revolution Mobil Yellow Fevers

NOT TO SCALE...

KEEP OUT

Paul - I've
added a few
changes
to disguise it.

"Border collies are intelligent, devoted, 'black and white' and are the best companions one could ever want. For me, it was pure unconditional love at its best."
Peter Brock

"Dougie (Douglas D. Dog) was a pup the family purchased from race fans in Queensland who named their kennels after Peter. The two developed an amazing bond and were inseparable when Peter was home. It was absolute devotion from both parties. Doug and Jazz (his sister) became part of the family when they first arrived on the farm in 1989. Peter could not bear to be present when Dougie had to be put to sleep in 2004. Peter buried him on top of the hill so he could look over his beloved farm, where he wanted his ashes to be spread."

Beverley Brock

Top – Peter with Dougie, Doori and Kiah on his outdoor setting. (Photo supplied by Beverley Brock used in the Herald Sun)

Right – Jamie and Peter with the family.

Opposite – The true Aussie icon – Peter complete with an Akubra, Tilly the Pet Kangaroo, Dougie and the Jackaroo.

"It is hard for many people to reconcile,

that a man credited with being Australia's top touring-car driver of all time would be interested in the gentler things of life. Such things as sketching, nature, meditation and, yes, even breeding tiny birds. It is easier to imagine that someone of Peter's ilk would spend his quiet moments watching Formula 1, reading action books or watching action movies. The

reality was far from that. Even as a young lad Peter, by his own admission, loved the bush. He appreciated the freedom of the wide open spaces and when out in nature would cast a watchful eye on the creatures that filled those places.

To refresh his body and soul in preparation for his next bout of frenetic activity, he tuned in to the Australian countryside. In each home we lived in, he'd build native gardens and aviaries, which he would painstakingly design and maintain. Our garden in Eltham was filled with rosellas and mountain lowrys, galahs and sulphur cresteds, lorikeets and corellas, kookaburras and magpies, finches of various types along with pardalotes and honey eaters, wattle birds, wrens and robins, as well as the delightful fantails. Peter would keep his numerous bird books handy

Above – Peter with a cup of herbal tea in the finch enclosure.

Opposite – The bird haven Peter created outside the lounge-room window in Eltham.

When the demands of Peter's hectic life had kept him away from his retreat for some time, it was not uncommon to find him just sitting on his specially-built seats in the orchards where he could watch the incessant activity of these tiny birds. More than anything he loved to watch them build their nests and protect their young. He would sketch the nests, intrigued by the innate way each species had to create their own unique style of nest. He would discuss just how nature had devised these superb ways to make the most of the niche they inhabited.

He hand-fed the wild birds on the verandah railings. The kookaburras would bang on the windows of a morning if they had not been fed. Seed bays were put out for the larger birds and smaller hanging feeders for the blue wrens, finches, pardalotes and silver eyes.

in case he saw a stranger come into his space. He would want to discover all he could to make sure he provided the right environment for it to keep coming back. He even named the property 'Carawah', an Aboriginal name which meant 'Birds come here to land'.

By the time the family had acquired the farm and moved on to 188 acres, he had totally committed to breeding up the numbers of finches that were once found naturally in the area. They had disappeared when most of the native bush was cleared for farming. His first mission was to plant thousands of trees and bushes to provide an adequate understory to attract and protect the birds when they either came or he released them.

The orchards needed to be netted to protect the fruit from the marauding cockatoos and the deer that wandered through the paddocks. These netted areas provided the perfect haven for breeding finches and so he spent many hours building suitable nesting sites among the fruit trees.

On one particular occasion, Peter had been watching some wrens build a delicate hanging nest in the bushes on the hillside. He had taken the family one by one around to look at the incredible workmanship and was keeping a watchful eye on the activity around the nest. He came home one day to find the nest torn apart, agitated parents flying around and a cat disappearing down the hillside. He was truly devastated.

Peter was an enigma. He was really one of the most gentle souls, who didn't seem to fit into the external world in which he excelled.

Beverley Brock

Top – The new aviaries built in Eltham.

Opposite – Bushwalking in Wilsons Promontory and feeding the crimson lowrys.

"PB came to Blackwater one day to see all his cars l had been collecting, sitting in my shed and said, 'Mate you have to show people these cars, it's fantastic!' Over the following five years the Brock Experience began to take shape. Peter Brock visited the site at Yeppoon in Queensland, and was instrumental in the planning of the tourist attraction.

On what was to be his final visit to Yeppoon in May 2006, he signed the front counter and drew some great pictures for ideas for the entrance.

When Peter was tragically killed in September 2006, the disbelief was just overwhelming. Through our own personal grief, we decided to push ahead with the Experience and see Brocky's dream come to life. Champion's Brock Experience was opened to the public in December 2007, 14 months after Peter's passing. From the

Top – Peter Brock and Peter Champion.

Above – Peter Brock sketching the entrance to the museum at his kitchen table.

Opposite – Peter Brock's cars at the museum.

(Photos supplied by Peter Champion)

| More of Peter's cars at the museum. (Photo supplied by Peter Champion)

amazing people we have met that have visited the experience since its inception, one thing comes through to us time and time again.

Peter Brock was a man of the people – yes he was an amazing racing-car driver, but the love of the fans was won from who he was as a person. He could teach many a young person today a lot about giving of themselves.

The Experience was developed out of passion, love and commitment not only from me and my wife, Sandy, along with our dedicated family and friends, but also the Brock family themselves. The passing of our friend Peter Brock was a great tragedy. He is still very much missed by all of us and we are blessed to be able to be amongst his many cars, achievements and memories. This private collection represents the very public life of the Australian Icon, Peter Brock and his 'Brocky magic'."

Peter Champion

(Brock collector and friend)

The Collection in Yeppoon, Queensland, has over 40 Peter Brock road and race cars, from his muscle car heritage HDT road cars through to the 82, 83 and 84 Bathurst winners. The very first car he raced at Bathurst in 1969 and the last car he raced at Bathurst, the VX Commodore, are also here. Along with a host of trophies, race suits, helmets and race paraphernalia there are also many original prints, framed awards and even some of Peter's own sketches. This really is a snapshot of not only the life of the legendary Peter Brock, but also of Australian motor racing history. Champion's Brock Experience is currently open by appointment only.

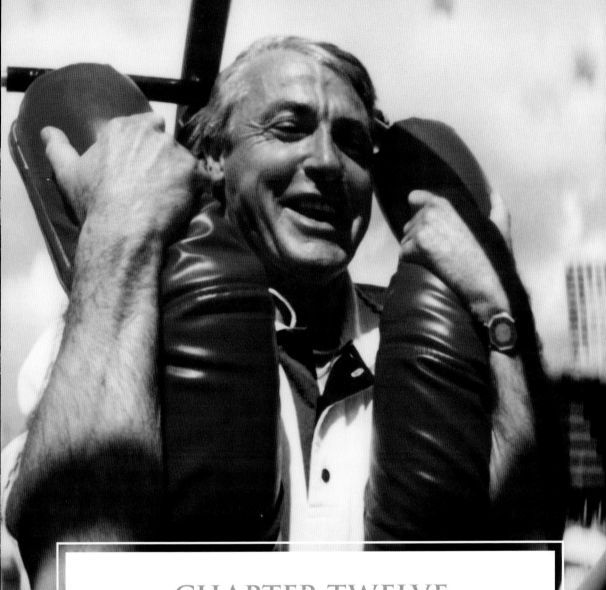

CHAPTER TWELVE

PETER'S PERSONAL PHOTO ALBUM

"We are all mere mortals trying our best, but I have been fortunate to meet some exceptional human beings in my time."

Brock Liam
Tuesday May 29th 2007
5.08am
377?? ?? - 8lb 5ozs
?cms - 20.5 inches

Enjoy life !

Peter Brock

PETER BROCK

1945–2006

To all Peter's fans...

The Brock family wishes to extend our deepest thanks and appreciation to all of you; it is gratifying to know that Peter still has the support of so many.

Thank you to everyone who has sent in letters and photos, and shared memories that make up this timeless book.

I know that Peter would want you to make the most of every moment of your lives – to take full responsibility for your choices and, above all, to take care on the roads!

Beverley Brock